THE TOTAL KEYBOARD PLAYER

A Guide to the Sounds, Styles & Sonic Spectrum

T0079193

for the musicians

THE TOTAL KEYBOARD PLAYER

A Guide to the Sounds, Styles & Sonic Spectrum

by Dave Adler

HAL•LEONARD® CORPORATION

7777 W. BLUEMOUND RD. P.O. BOX 13819 MILWAUKEE, WI 53213

ISBN 978-1-4234-7604-7

In Australia Contact:
Hal Leonard Australia Pty. Ltd.
4 Lentara Court
Cheltenham, Victoria, 3192 Australia
Email: ausadmin@halleonard.com.au

Printed in the U.S.A.

First Edition

Visit Hal Leonard Online at
www.halleonard.com

CONTENTS

PREFACE

July 1969. I've just turned four and my parents have taken me to Shakey's Pizza to celebrate. In the center of the restaurant a man wearing a straw hat is playing Ragtime piano. I'm mesmerized. The sounds pouring out of this magical box fill me with awe, joy, and wonder. It's a turning point in my life. From that moment on, all I will ever really want to be is a keyboard player.

My fascination with this wonderful instrument convinces my very supportive parents to enroll me in classical piano lessons, and for the next ten years I practice every day. During this formative period I learn to read music, play the major and minor scales, and absorb the basic fundamentals of theory and technique upon which I still rely. I perform at student recitals and learn to sight read. Somewhere along the line I begin to improvise and make up tunes. I discover I can impress my peers by playing the latest hits. Music is something that comes very easily and naturally to me. This is truly a blessing, as I'm otherwise completely uncoordinated, terrible at sports, and an average student. The more that time passes, the more I realize that keyboards are my ticket to self-actualization.

A few years later I purchase my first electronic keyboard, a Lowrey T-1 portable organ. I'm thrilled with the other-worldly sounds it produces. I start imitating my favorite players: Ray Manzarek of the Doors, John Lord of Deep Purple, and Gregg Rolie of Santana. Their lead lines and comping patterns enthrall me. I soak up their individual styles, listening to the parts over and over until I've completely absorbed them. I strive to emulate every note and flourish. More and more I find myself gravitating toward the free-wheeling, highly emotive, uninhibited style of rock and roll. I yearn to play music with others, to share the euphoria and magical collective experience that only jamming with fellow musicians can bring.

I start watching classic concert films: Woodstock, Monterey Pop Festival, Pink Floyd at Pompeii. The keyboard players in these bands all make vital contributions to their respective ensembles, and each of them seems to be having a great time while they're at it. Free, uninhibited, and seemingly effortless in style and manner, they establish their own musical identities while making important additions to the whole. I marvel at their compelling vocabulary of sounds, virtuosic runs, and undaunted sense of fun.

I start jamming with my friend Paul Lottridge on drums. Our first number is "Cars" by Gary Numan. I hold down the bass line with my left hand while playing the signature string line with my right. I discover that by running my organ through a phasor, the tone becomes filtered in a magical, compelling manner. I can't believe that this simple little box puts me in the same sonic space as the players I idolize.

In high school Paul and I team up with our friends Eric Hailman and Chris Laine on guitar and bass, and all of a sudden I'm in a real live rock band. Our peers, who previously had never given us the time of day, now ask us to perform at dances and parties. We become popular among the popular set, something I never imagined happening in my wildest dreams. This music thing seems to be working out pretty well.

I start adding other keyboards to my arsenal: A Korg CX enables me to mimic that wonderful, classic Hammond/Leslie organ sound. A Korg Poly 800 yields mind-blowing synth patches. A Wurlitzer electric piano makes even the most basic of parts feel funky and groovalicious.

The musical give-and-take of the band teaches me when to solo and when to hold back, how to use rhythm and percussive playing to mimic the guitar, and about the important role pacing and subtlety play in making an understated yet substantial contribution to the overall sound. As a stationary instrument, I cannot hope to approach the freedom of movement and audience intimacy enjoyed by my guitar-playing counterparts. I learn, however, that by incorporating body language, carefully watching and reacting to the other players, musically supporting and soloing as needed, and tastefully exploiting the instruments' countless sonic textures, I can function on equal terms as a vital and exciting performer and band member. The kids cheer! One night we each make 50 bucks—we're rich! I've finally found my place in the world.

I decide to pursue my musical studies in college, but the solitude brought on by hour upon hour spent alone in a practice room starts bringing me down. I miss the fun, spontaneity, and camaraderie of playing with my mates. Music had always been an escape for me; now it has become a chore. After a year I switch my major to English.

But I don't stop playing. Pick-up gigs in country bands and Top 40 outfits pay my rent. (They still do, come to think of it.) I move from one different group to the next, each experience contributing to my general sense of expression and individual style. Performing is a riot—I love watching the crowd move and react to the notes I choose.

Enticed by the promise of fame and fortune, my bandmates (Rod Halverson and Sam Schneidman) and I move to Chicago to chase down our destiny. While initially enticed by the city that calls itself "home of the blues," I soon find myself accompanying actors within the city's vital improv-theatre scene. I learn to trust my instincts, go with the flow, not censor. My past studies of different musical genres inform and compel my playing as I make up songs and underscore scenes written and performed on-the-spot by the talented performers. I discover that the keyboard functions well not only within the world of the musical ensemble, but also that of the dramatic and theatrical. I can even incorporate humor into my playing, cracking up audiences with topical musical references, over-emphasized emotions, and heightened musical reactions. The keyboards facilitate my ability to freely and immediately comment, in an engaging and supportive manner, upon whatever is happening onstage at the moment.

Initially music had been my ticket to self-realization; now I was a "real pro," moving and shaking in the big city and jamming with up-and-comers in the comedy circuit who, years later, would become popular stars of stage and screen.

Over the next several years my stints would lead to myriad unforgettable and life-changing experiences. I lived in Austin for a year and soaked up the inde-music scene. In Los Angeles I completed USC's esteemed composition program specializing in scoring for motion pictures and television, and worked as a composer's assistant. In New York City I scored a season of *Upright Citizens Brigade*, a sketch-comedy show, for Comedy Central. I served as musical director and arranger for Richard Cheese, a brilliant performer who fused classic lounge stylings with alternative rock; we were regulars in Vegas and toured the coasts. I made records with innumerable local bands. With my good friend Willy Porter, a gifted guitarist and songwriter from Milwaukee, I helped write, arrange, and record five CDs. I scored indie films, wrote string arrangements, and played countless concerts. All the while my fascination with the keyboard never waned, each experience leading me to new sonic discoveries and musical insights.

My work as a keyboardist, arranger, and composer has been and remains for me an ever-present source of joy, inspiration, love, and gratitude. My musical sense of wonder never falters. Supporting the song, harmonically commenting on lyrics, reacting to the crowd, manipulating and exploiting energy to positive effect: these have become my stock-in-trade as a keyboard player. The instrument perpetually fuels my desire to act as a conduit though which a greater and infinitely more dynamic energy can flow.

As I keep playing and learning, my vocabulary of sounds, licks, and melody lines continues to expand. A keyboard player can make a good band great, and a great band stellar. Emotionally we can heighten the impact of a beautiful song, provide a lush bed upon which others can solo and groove, or give a jam that special extra lift or push that can drive an audience crazy—in a good way. In the studio, the counterpoint and sonic balance that keyboards provide can add that indefinable, essential musical spice that makes a track shimmer. The more I absorb, the better my ability to make these things happen.

The keys have proven to be my key to musical and self-fulfillment. The low, thunderous roar of the Hammond, the undeniable funkiness of the Clavinet, the smooth, sophisticated timbre of the Fender Rhodes, and the down-home, soul-fuelled vibe of the acoustic piano—these are the sounds and styles that never fail to thrill and inspire me. It is my sincere hope that this book will facilitate other aspiring players to experience their own levels of joy, wonder, and musical satisfaction.

I am thankful, proud, honored, and lucky to be a musician! Rock on!

—Dave Adler

INTRODUCTION

WHO THE...

Who is this guy? That's probably the first thing you thought when you picked up this book. Maybe you're a working musician who's looking for a few good tips, or someone who's just thinking about joining a band for the first time. You're a keyboard player, heir of a righteous breed. You love to rock, and you live to lay it down. You saw this book somewhere and you thought, "This looks interesting." Well let me tell you, my fellow musical sojourner, that fate and the finely tuned synergy of the stars have led you to this page, and you're reading exactly the right words at precisely the right time.

Who I am isn't really important; let me tell you about what I do. I live, sleep, eat, and breathe keyboards every moment of every day of my life. I've tuned pianos that went south under hot lights, convinced strangers to help lug my Hammond, fished for solder fillings in the belly of a Wurly, hoisted a Rhodes Suitcase piano up countless staircases, and played organ under the northern lights of Kodiak, Alaska. I've returned rentals so bloody with hand-abuse that I've been charged a cleaning fee. I've driven to scary, remote locations in the hopes of procuring rare vintage gear. I've lived in sonic trenches and fought at the Battle of Amplitude. I worship at the altar of KORG, eat at the Yamaha Diner, seek medical attention at MOOG Hospital, and sleep at the Steinway Hotel. In other words, if it's a keyboard, I've amped it, champed it, revamped it, and double-stamped it. Keyboards are my life.

Here's what you can expect from this book: a frank, passionate, inside-the-circle, under-the-rope and outside-the-box keyboardic testimonial; all the lessons, secrets, tips, voicings, tricks, starts, go-tos, and patches that I've been fortunate enough to pick up on the road, in the studio, and in the field as a 100 percent certified professional, working keyboardist, composer, arranger, and producer. I've played big houses and small clubs all over the world, and even went through a short-lived "keyboard tie" phase. My range of experience includes live playing, keyboard repair, film scoring, music editing, engineering, and session work. This will be a musical tell-all that actually tells it all like it is: the good, the bad, and the harmonious. A complete, all-encompassing, keycentric compendium written by and for keyboardists.

And, hopefully and most importantly, this book will help you become a better player.

As someone who's been lucky and blessed enough to follow a musical path, I'm also driven to write this book so that the music might live on. What we do is vital and essential. We're the purveyors of energy and light. We can play the symphony of life and transpose it to fit whatever key the cosmic choir requires. I live to serve the music, and by passing along the insights and lessons I've been able to experience and learn, I hope to aid and inspire other like-minded players out there, those who also live and work to insure that the sacred torch of skillful playing and quality performance remains forever well-lit.

KEY DISCLOSURE

This is my book. It's based on my point of view formulated by my genetic makeup and my experience of the world. Theses are my opinions, rules, observations, conclusions, and biases. This is what has worked for me, Dave Adler, professional keyboard player. I'm passing these observations on to you in the hope that some of them will help, but doubtless, as a fellow voyager of this modern world, you will chart your own course and go with whatever works for you.

HOW THE...

1. This book is composed of words and sounds. It is organized into chapters for handy reference.

2. Read the words and listen to the sounds.

3. "Have a good time all the time."

—Ross MacLochness
(*Spinal Tap* keyboardist)

WHY THE...

Why play the keyboards? Because, at their best, they can function as an effective musical facilitator, providing harmonic context to support the sonic story. Or, they can shine as a bright, forceful solo voice. Their infinite tonal possibilities present the player with the most varied and compelling of musical palates. Truly, they are a limitlessly inspiring and versatile musical tool.

WHAT THE...

What are the prerequisites for being a top-notch keyboard player? Here's a slightly edited version of what the National Association for Music Education has to say:

> Your background and education are important for a career as a performer, but usually not as significant as talent, persistence, showmanship, and a little luck. Emotional maturity is another prerequisite and, of course, music training is definitely helpful. In pop, rock, and jazz the ear is and should be of prime importance; as an instrumentalist, you should be able to execute what you hear. The musician who succeeds is the one who has mastered the technique of satisfying the particular audience he or she is aiming for, while not compromising his or her personal, unique vision and sound. Consequently, it is important that you expand your musical orbit by carefully listening to a wide variety of music, as these influences can provide ideas and inspiration for you. High level of energy and an ability to entertain is required.

I more or less agree with this, although they fail to mention some vital skill-sets, including good night vision and duct-tape malleability.

KEY AND BOARDER

In the criminal music system, the keyboard player is represented by two separate yet equally important groups: tone, which establishes the all-important and ever-transcendent vibe, and presence, which is the physical manifestation of spirit and the conduit of soul power here on good ol' Earth. These are their stories.

Tone: The idea is to define exactly which sounds best represent the message and intent of the music you're playing, followed by the best possible instrument that serves those needs. Real (i.e., vintage) instruments are almost always better, although they're usually very heavy and more expensive, so much of the time you'll have to find a synth or sampler that "goes for it" the hardest. This is where it all starts.

Presence: The complexity (or preferably, the simplicity) of your rig, the clothes you wear, your conduct and demeanor onstage; all of those things contribute to how the audience will perceive YOU, and thereby your music. We can't do cartwheels like guitar players. We're not hitting things with clubs like drummers. We're standing (or sitting) in front of an assembly of black and white buttons and shiny metal knobs, housed in an awkward looking box-like container. The audience sees you flailing away at what appears to them to be a hotel mini-bar. This is what we have to work with, but it's more than enough to rock out and fit in.

Personally, I try to keep it simple. This includes my rig and my clothes. From there I trust my musical instincts and dance constantly.

KEYS TO THE KINGDOM

You can play lightning-fast arpeggios or slow, gorgeous melody lines, diminished sevenths or augmented fifths, with great flourish or quiet simplicity; in the end the only thing that really matters, both onstage and in the studio, is your level of commitment: to the music, to the part you're playing in its creation, and to the inspirational energy that informs and directs your musical choices.

I find that the more I surrender myself (ergo, my ego) to the music, the more likely and conducive it is to "zone" playing, which is basically the ultimate manifestation of full and ultimate surrender to a higher musical power.

REELIN' IN THE KEYS

Like watts through a power strip, so are the boards of our lives. Here's an astoundingly brief and biased history of keyboard development through the ages:

3rd century B.C. – Greek engineer Ctesibius creates single-manual, slider-chest organ (hydraulis) powered by a piston pump that supplies air to a reservoir.

1st century A.D. – Roman architect Vitruvius describes an organ with balanced keys.

2nd century A.D. – The pumps and water regulators of the hydraulis are gradually replaced by an inflated leather bag. Hero of Alexandria builds pipe organ.

7th century – First appearance of bellows-powered organ.

11th century – Italian music theorist Guido of Arezzo applies the keyboard to stringed instruments. Develops modern musical notation on the side.

14th century – First appearance of the clavichord. When a key is pressed, a metal tangent strikes the corresponding string from below.

15th century – First appearance of the harpsichord, which uses a bird quill or a piece of hard leather (referred to as the plectrum) to pluck its strings.

1700 – Introduction of equal temperament (also circular or circulating temperament). The twelve notes per octave are tuned in such a way that it is now possible to play music in all major and minor keys without sounding perceptibly out of tune.

1709 – Italian harpsichord maker Bartolomeo Cristofori replaces picks with hammers, enabling musicians to play the instrument dynamically. He calls his invention a "gravicembalo col piano e forte" (harpsichord with soft and loud). The name is shortened to "pianoforte" and eventually just "piano."

1828 – Ignaz Bösendorfer begins manufacturing pianos in Vienna.

1840 – Alexandre Debain invents first reed organ (harmonium) in Paris.

1853 – German immigrant Heinrich Engelhard Steinweg (later Henry E. Steinway) founds Steinway & Sons in New York City.

1857 – Matthias Hohner founds Hohner Musical Instruments in Trossingen, Germany.

1876 – Elisha Gray invents first synthesizer (the "musical telegraph"), a chance by-product of telephone technology.

1886 – W.W. Kimball introduces initial line of pianos and organs.

1900 – Torakusu Yamaha builds Japan's first piano.

1918 – Frederick C. Lowrey builds prototype of electronic organ.

Early 1930s – New York inventor Benjamin F. Miessner designs amplified conventional upright piano.

1934 – Laurens Hammond patents Model A organ.

1946 – Harold Rhodes invents the Rhodes Electric Piano.

1950s – Ivory discontinued on all makes of American pianos. Hohner releases Melodica.

1955 – Introduction of Wurlitzer electric piano.

1956 – California inventor Harry Chamberlin invents an electro-mechanical keyboard instrument that incorporates individual tape loops for each note (the "Chamberlin"). Precursor to the English Mellotron.

1962 – Vox introduces the Continental Combo organ.

1964 – Hohner introduces the Clavinet. Farfisa introduces the Combo Compact organ.

1965 – Introduction of Fender Rhodes electric piano; invented by Harold Rhodes in an effort to create a piano that injured soldiers can play while lying in a hospital bed.

1967 – Robert Moog introduces first Moog synthesizer, the 900 Series.

1968 – Wendy Carlos popularizes Moog via chart-topping album *Switched-On Bach*.

1969 – EMS releases the VCS 3 (Voltage Controlled Studio with 3 oscillators) portable analog synthesizer.

1970s – Alan Robert Pearlman founds ARP Instruments.

1971 – Moog introduces the Minimoog synthesizer, designed to incorporate the most important parts of a modular synthesizer into a compact unit with no need for patch cords.

1973 – Korg releases the MiniKorg, its first synthesizer. Tom Oberheim founds Oberheim Electronics.

1975 – New England Digital releases the Synclavier synthesizer/sampler.

1976 – Yamaha develops the first polyphonic synthesizer.

1977 – Sequential Circuits releases the Prophet-5 synthesizer. English inventor Lesley Symons invents the Keytar.

1978 – Fairlight releases the CMI (Computer Musical Instrument) sampling synthesizer.

1979 – Korg introduces the CX-3, one of the earliest and (in my opinion) most authentic-sounding Hammond B-3 organ clones ever produced.

1980 – Casio releases the Casiotone keyboard instrument.

1981 – Korg releases the Polysix synthesizer.

1983 – Sequential Circuits founder Dave Smith introduces MIDI (Musical Instrument Digital Interface). Yamaha releases the DX7, the first widely popular digital synthesizer. Korg releases the Poly-800, the first fully programmable synthesizer that sells for less than $1,000.

1984 – Ensoniq introduces the Mirage, an eight-bit sampler priced below $2,000. Roland introduces the Juno-106 synthesizer. Kurzweil introduces the K250 synthesizer.

You'll notice my timeline stops at 1984. Why? Two reasons:

1. Redundancy. In my opinion, after 1984 the major focus of the technology of instrument development shifted from the advent of new sounds to ease of use and portability. This, combined with the newly found ability to sample sounds (which, in its own way, hastened the nostalgic focus of the collective ear) led to the current industry trends of today. It was now possible to fit the sounds of a Hammond, piano, and a whole bank of synths into one portable, user-friendly unit. As the collective cultural sonic vocabulary became established, a specific shift from sonics to electronics also took place. As time went on, the faithful reproduction of sounds and ease-of-use of the instrument became more and more advanced and sophisticated, leading ultimately to the "workstations" and "plug-ins" of today. When I listen to what's out there now I hear digitally based computer programs doing their level best, with varying degrees of success, to capture the vibe and essence of the vintage stuff, along with a few well-established acoustic instruments.

2. MIDI. With the universal popularization of MIDI it was now possible for someone with no actual playing ability to render usable, proficient keyboard parts via a sequencer. In my view this development was akin to what Ray Kurzweil (recognize that name?) refers to as the coming of the ultimate singularity, a time when technology will make it possible for anyone with a creative thought to have it rendered instantly and exactly as they imagine, with no need for any bothersome middlemen (us musicians, artists, writers, et al.).

But that's not going to happen for a while.

KEY BOARDS

The gear that made Milwaukee famous!

PIANO

COMMON NAME
Piano

FULL NAME
Gravicembalo col piano e forte
(Harpsichord with soft and loud)

ALIAS
the 88s
the Ivories
the Black and Whites
"An elaborate percussion instrument."
(Frank Zappa)

A.K.A.
Bösendorfer, Steinway, Yamaha, various

YEAR OF ORIGIN
1709

PLACE OF ORIGIN
Padua, Italy

Piano

SONIC SOURCE
Depression of key triggers hammer that strikes one, two, or three strings simultaneously. Felt damper mechanism ceases string vibration upon release. Moving parts responsible for striking strings collectively called the "action."

DESCRIPTION
88 keys. Over 9,000 parts. 230 strings (average); length, thickness, and tension determine pitch. "Constructive interference" (two or more unison strings vibrating together) increases volume and warmth. "Beats" are perceived variations in volume produced by two or more strings vibrating slightly out of tune.

Upper 60 notes employ three strings per note, middle 18 two strings per note, lower 10 one string per note. Strings are made of steel wire; bass strings are wrapped with copper or iron winding to add weight and thickness. Total tension in a concert grand is about 30 tons. Strings held in place by cast iron plate and tuned by lessening or increasing tension via metal pins on mounted on pinblock, which is generally constructed from laminated maple to counter tension. Soundboard frequently made of spruce due to the wood's highly resonant qualities.

Types
Spinet (as little as three feet long)
Console (about 42 inches long)
Upright (about 51 inches long)
Baby grand: (nearly 6 feet long)
Professional grand (6 feet long)
Concert grand (nearly 9 feet long)

Pedals
Right: "damper," sustains tone via disengagement of dampers. Most commonly used pedal.
Middle: "sostenuto," sustains only those notes played at time of depression.
Left: "una corda," shifts action to decrease number of strings per note struck by hammer.

BACKGROUND
Invented in 1709 by Bartolomeo Cristofori (1655–1731), a harpsichord maker and instrument curator for the Medici family. German keyboard builder Gottfried Siberman (1683–1753) added the damper pedal in 1725. The ability to produce rapidly repeated notes ("double escapement") was introduced in 1821 by Sebastian Erard (1752–1831).

ACCOMPLICES
Helpinstill: Roadmaster; Portable Grand; renowned piano pickup manufacturer
Kurzweil: K2000 series
Native Instruments: Akoustik Piano
Roland: RD series
Yamaha: Clavinova, CP-70, CP-80, S-80

KEY PLAYERS
Blues/Boogie-Woogie/Ragtime/Stride
Albert Ammons, Jimmy Blythe, Charles Brown, Charles "Cow-Cow" Davenport, Blind John Davis, Champion Jack Dupree, Cecil Grant, Henry Gray, James P. Johnson, Pete Johnson, Scott Joplin, Detroit Junior, Meade Lux Lewis, Amos Milburn, Little Brother Montgomery, Jelly Roll Morton, Pinetop Perkins, Lucky Roberts, Sunnyland Slim, Memphis Slim, Pinetop Smith, Willie "the Lion" Smith, Otis Spann, Roosevelt Sykes, George W. Thomas, Fats Waller, Jimmy Yancey.

Classical
George Antheil, Emanuel Ax, Johann Sebastian Bach, Bela Bartok, Ludwig van Beethoven, Leonard Bernstein, Nadia Boulanger, Johannes Brahms, John Cage, Frederic Chopin, Muzio Clementi, Van Cliburn, Claude Debussy, Antonin Dvořák, Glenn Gould, Edvard Grieg, Joseph Haydn, Vladamir Horowitz, Gyorgy Ligeti, Franz Liszt, Felix Mendelssohn, Wolfgang Amadeus Mozart, André Previn, Sergei Prokofiev, Sergei Rachmaninoff, Maurice Ravel, Arthur Rubinstein, Camille Saint-Saëns, Erik Satie, Domenico Scarlatti, Franz Schubert, Robert Schumann, Peter and Rudolf Serkin, Jeffrey Siegel, Dmitri Shostakovich, Pyotr Ilyich Tchaikovsky, Andre Watts.

Jazz
Toshiko Akiyoshi, Count Basie, James Beard, Dave Brubeck, Nat "King" Cole, Harry Connick Jr., Chick Corea, Rich Dworsky, Duke Ellington, Bill Evans, Gil Evans, Victor Feldman, George Gershwin, Dave Grusin, Herbie Hancock, Laurence Hobgood, Dick Hyman, Ahmad Jamal, Keith Jarrett, Stan Kenton, Kenny Kirkland, Oscar Levant, Lyle Mays, Marian McPartland, Thelonious Monk, Oscar Peterson, Bud Powell, Sun-Ra, Ben Sidran, Horace Silver, Billy Strayhorn, Art Tatum, McCoy Tyner, Hiromi Uehara, Fats Waller.

Rock
Michael Bearden, Roy Bittan, James Brown, David Bryan, Ray Charles, Jon Cleary, Commander Cody, Dennis DeYoung, Fats Domino, Ben Folds, Craig Frost, Aretha Franklin, Johnny Griffith, Jules Holland, Nicky Hopkins, Bruce Hornsby, Joe Hunter, Billy Joel, Elton John, Dr. John, Johnnie Johnson, Al Kooper, Carole King, Chuck Leavell, John Lennon, Jerry Lee Lewis, Ramsey Lewis, Professor Longhair, Richard Manuel, Paul McCartney, Ian McLagan, Freddie Mercury, Randy Newman, Bill Payne, Steve Pocaro, Billy Powell, Little Richard, Leon Russell, Todd Rundgren, Paul Shaffer, Chris Stainton, Ian Stewart, Richard Tee, Pete Townshend, Alan Toussaint, Earl Van Dyke, Bobby Whitlock, Steve Winwood, Stevie Wonder, Richard Wright, Neil Young.

Additional players
Victor Borge
Richard Clayderman
Liberace
Chico Marx

EAR WITNESS
The ultimate sonic paintbrush. The one that got me started. Untamable. Approach with reverence.

HAMMOND B-3 ELECTRIC ORGAN

COMMON NAME
B-3

FULL NAME
Hammond B-3 Electric Organ

ALIAS
C-3 (B-3 with "modesty panels," intended for church use), M-3 (smaller version of B-3, less range/ no presets) et al.

A.K.A.
Suzuki (acquired Hammond in 1989)

YEAR OF ORIGIN
1934

PLACE OF ORIGIN
Evanston, Illinois

Hammond B-3 Electric Organ

SONIC SOURCE
Synchronous motor (operates at fixed number of rotations per minute) turns 95 coin-sized tonewheels, each of which is individually cut to determine pitch and waveform (sine). Tonewheels originally made of Bakelite, an early plastic, to eliminate noise. Closely placed, lightly charged magnetic pickups facilitate transduction of generated frequencies (91 total).

DESCRIPTION
Two manuals: swell (upper) and great (lower). Set of nine drawbars ("stops") enables addition of harmonics to fundamental pitches. Numbers on drawbars based on pipe organ footage system. Pulling drawbar out increases volume of corresponding frequency, reference numbers on bars enable marking of settings. Four sets of drawbars enable two settings for each manual, along with an additional limited set for optional bass pedals. Black and white keys at the left of both manuals allow for an additional 10 drawbar presets per manual.

Drawbar layout
brown, 16', down 1 octave from fundamental
brown, 5-1/3', up perfect fifth from fundamental
white, 8', fundamental
white, 4', up 1 octave from fundamental
black, 2-2/3', up 1 octave + perfect 5th from fundamental
white, 2', up 2 octaves from fundamental
black, 1-3/5', up 2 octaves + major 3rd from fundamental
black, 1-1/3', up 2 octaves + perfect 5th from fundamental
white, 1', up 3 octaves from fundamental

Panel Controls

"start" and "run" switches – start/maintain motor operation

volume – soft/normal
(Volume also controlled via foot-operated pedal)
vibrato/swell – on/off
vibrato/great – on/off
vibrato/chorus – type select

percussion – on/off (amplifies selected upper frequency)
percussion – volume (soft/norm)
percussion – decay (fast/slow)
percussion – harmonic select (2nd, 3rd)

Leslie Organ Speaker

Integrated speaker/amplification system; vented enclosure houses rotating speaker and high-frequency horn. Doppler effect adds tremolo, chorus, and pitch-shift to signal. Variable speeds (fast/slow/off) triggered via footswitch or controls mounted below lower manual.

Overdrive effect can be added through manipulation of expression pedal, internal tone control, and/or Leslie speaker preamp setting.

Customized cutaway or "chop" versions (keyboard separated from guts) designed for portability.

BACKGROUND

Invented by Laurens Hammond (1895–1973), who patented the Model A on April 24, 1934. Claimed his instrument could generate 253 million different possible tones!

The B-3 and C-3 series were manufactured from 1954 to 1974.

The M-3 series was manufactured from 1955 to 1964.

The singular "key click" sound was originally considered an annoyance.
(The L-100 series attempted to remedy this.)

Leslie organ speaker invented by Donald J. Leslie (1913–2004).

ACCOMPLICES

Crummar: Organizer
Farfisa: Compact; Compact Duo; Professional; VIP
Hammond/Suzuki: XK-3c
Harmonium/Reed Organ/Pump Organ
Korg: CX-3; BX-3
Lowrey: Heritage Deluxe; Festival
Motion Sound: various Leslie clones
Native Instruments: B4 II
Nord: C-2; Electro 2
Pipe Organ
Vox: Continental; Jaguar
Yamaha: SK 30

KEY PLAYERS *(GOSPEL, JAZZ, BLUES, ROCK)*

HAMMOND

Akkerman, Jan/Focus, "Hocus Pocus" (1971)

Argent, Rod/The Zombies, "Time of the Season" (1967)

Argent, Rod/Argent, "Hold Your Head Up" (1972)

Allman, Gregg/The Allman Brothers Band, "Whipping Post" (1969)

Banks, Tony/Genesis, "The Lamb Lies Down on Broadway" (1974)

Brown, James/"The Funky Drummer" (1969)

Boyd, Roger/Head East, "Never Been Any Reason" (1975)

Cavaliere, Felix/The Young Rascals, "Good Lovin'" (1966)

Corbetta, Jerry/Sugarloaf, "Green-Eyed Lady" (1970)

Emerson, Keith/ELP, "Karn Evil 9" (1973)

Evan, John/Jethro Tull, "Aqualung" (1971)

Federici, Danny/Bruce Springsteen & the E Street Band, "Hungry Heart" (1980)

Fisher, Matthew/Procol Harum, "A Whiter Shade of Pale" (1967)

Galuten, Albhy/Eric Clapton, "I Shot the Sheriff" (1974)

Kooper, Al/Bob Dylan, "Like a Rolling Stone" (1965)

Harvey, Bernard "Touter"/Bob Marley, "No Woman No Cry" (1974)

Hodges, Charles/Al Green, "Let's Stay Together" (1972)

Holmes, Richard "Groove," "Groovin' for Mr. G." (1971)

Jones, John Paul/Led Zeppelin, "You're Time Is Gonna Come" (1969)

Lord, Jon/Deep Purple, "Hush" (1968)

McDuff, "Brother" Jack, "Blues and Tonic" (1961)

McGriff, Jimmy, "I Got a Woman" (1962)

McJohn, Goldy/Steppenwolf, "Magic Carpet Ride" (1968)

McKernan, Ron "Pigpen"/The Grateful Dead, "Playing in the Band" (1971)

McVie, Christine/Fleetwood Mac, "Over My Head" (1975)

Neville, Art/The Meters, "Tippi-Toes" (1970)

Preston, Billy, "Will It Go Round in Circles" (1973)

Rolie, Gregg/Santana, "Soul Sacrifice" (1969)

Scholz, Tom/Boston, "Foreplay/Long Time" (1976)

Smith, Jimmy, "The Sermon" (1958)

Smith, Lonnie, "Hola Muneca" (1967)

Smith, Robert/The Cure, "10:15 Saturday Night" (1979)

Stills, Steven, "Love the One You're With" (1970)

Stone, Sly/Sly & The Family Stone, "Dance to the Music" (1968)

T., Booker/Booker T. & the MG's, "Green Onions" (1962)

Tench, Benmont/Tom Petty and the Heartbreakers, "Refugee" (1980)

Wakeman, Rick/Yes, "Roundabout" (1971)

Winwood, Stevie/Spencer Davis Group, "Gimme Some Loving" (1967)

Wright, Dan/Kansas, "Carry On, Wayward Son" (1977)

Wright, Richard/Pink Floyd, "Shine On, You Crazy Diamond" (1975)

Wynans, Reese/Stevie Ray Vaughan & Double Trouble, "Look at Little Sister" (1985)

Young, Joachim/Steve Miller, "Fly Like an Eagle" (1976)

Additional players

DeFrancesco, Joey

Medeski, John

FARFISA

Humphrey, Fred/The Pharoahs, "Wooly Bully" (1965)

Oldham, Spooner/Percy Sledge, "When a Man Loves a Woman" (1966)

Weitz, Mark/Strawberry Alarm Clock, "Incense and Peppermints" (1967)

Wright, Richard/Pink Floyd, "Set the Controls for the Heart of the Sun" (1968)

LOWREY

Hudson, Garth/The Band, "Chest Fever" (1968)

McCartney, Paul/The Beatles, "Lucy in the Sky with Diamonds" (1967)

Townshend, Pete/The Who, "Baba O'Riley" (1971)

PIPE ORGAN

DeYoung, Dennis/Styx, "Blue Collar Man" (1978)

VOX

Ingle, Doug/Iron Butterfly, "In-a-Gadda-Da-Vida" (1968)

Manzarek, Ray/The Doors, "Light My Fire" (1967)

Nieve, Steve/Elvis Costello & The Attractions, "Radio Radio" (1978)

Price, Alan/The Animals, "House of the Rising Sun" (1964)

Rodriquez, Frank/? & the Mysterians, "96 Tears" (1966)

Smith, Mike/The Dave Clark Five, "Bits & Pieces" (1964)

EAR WITNESS

Nothing rocks like a Hammond! It operates by its own set of rules. Used best when defining and occupying the available unused sonic space within a track. The left hand functions mainly as a sonic foil for the right—unless, of course, it's playing a bass line. Responds well to percussive accents and precise, specific part execution.

Glissandos are great to "woosh" your way up to and down from a note by holding down as many notes as possible with your left hand on your way up to or down from a targeted note.

The bass pedals can operate as a third manual, provided your feet are up to it.

I used to work with these beauties all the time until my mates got tired of hauling them around.

MELLOTRON KEYBOARD

COMMON NAME
Mellotron

FULL NAME
Mellotron Keyboard Driven Tape Replay Instrument

ALIAS
Chamberlin

A.K.A.
Novation

YEAR OF ORIGN
1956

PLACE OF ORIGIN
Iowa, Wisconsin

SONIC SOURCE
Depression of key triggers pinch roller, which touches rotating spindle and draws magnetic tape over replay head. Tape kept in place via pressure pad. Spring-return system rewinds tape back to original position.

DESCRIPTION
This single-manual keyboard came preloaded with three sounds per interchangeable tape frame. Each tape segment had a maximum length of eight seconds before the sample ran out. Players, however, appreciated the strength of the individual attacks of the sounds, made possible by the instrument's singular tape-return system. Common favorite sounds included strings, choirs, bass, and flute.

Mellotron Keyboard Driven Tape Replay Instrument

BACKGROUND
Harry Chamberlin, an organist and inventor, began experimenting with tape replay instruments around 1947 when he introduced the Rhythmate, one of the earliest drum machines. The keyboard driven Chamberlin was conjured in 1956. It is arguably the first sampler ever made. The instrument could hold a maximum of eight sounds, which were performed by members of Lawrence Welk's orchestra. Unique, high-quality tones were developed though the incorporation of these excellent players, each recorded individually in isolation, combined with Chamberlin's use of a Neumann U47 microphone and other top-of-the-line recording equipment. The key-triggered sounds could be played back at normal speed or manipulated by slowing down the tape as it passed over the replay heads, resulting in an unnaturally lower tone. Welk was impressed enough to offer to fund the instrument's development if renamed the "Welk," but Chamberlin declined.

Chamberlin sent his sales agent, Bill Fransen, overseas to purchase 70 matching tape heads. Upon meeting with the Bradley brothers, owners of Bradmatic Ltd. (later Streetly Electronics) in Birmingham, England, Fransen found both a supplier and a willing partner in crime. The group pirated Chamberlin's idea and began working on production of an instrument that incorporated the same principles as the Chamberlin, beginning with said tape heads in 1962. In 1964 they unveiled their "new" instrument: the Mellotron Mark I, so named through the union of Melo(dy) and (elec)Tron(ics). They followed up one year later with the updated Mellotron MK II.

These early instruments featured two side-by-side manuals, the left meant for rhythm and accompaniment and the right for melody. Each key triggered a matching 3/8-inch, 42 foot-long piece of magnetic tape. Each piece of tape held 18 different notes or passages, including performances from single acoustic instruments as well as jazz bands, string quartets, and choirs. All sections were performed in each relevant key.

Mike Pinder (of the Moody Blues), an early employee of Streetly Electronics, introduced the instrument to the Beatles in the mid '60s.

The Model 400, Mellotron's most widely popular instrument, was introduced in 1970. While the instrument was well constructed and its 3/4" recording tape interchangeable with 1/2", the sounds lacked the quality and subtlety of Chamberlin's original recordings. The two rival parties eventually agreed to coexist. Chamberlin focused on the American market, while Mellotronics, Mellotron's marketing and sales arm, concentrated its attention on Europe.

The fragility and unreliability of the Mellotron eventually lead to the instrument's demise.

ACCOMPLICES
CarbonAUHost: M-Tron

Optigan

KEY PLAYERS
Gaye, Marvin, "Mercy Mercy Me (The Ecology)" (1971)
Jones, John Paul/Led Zeppelin, "Kashmir" (1975)
McCartney, Paul/The Beatles, "Strawberry Fields Forever" (1967)
McDonald, Ian/King Crimson, "The Court of the Crimson King" (1969)
Jones, Brian/The Rolling Stones, "2000 Light Years from Home" (1967)
Parsons, Alan/The Alan Parsons Project, "I, Robot" (1977)
Pappalardi, Felix/Cream, "Badge" (1969)
Pinder, Mike/The Moody Blues, "Nights in White Satin" (1967)
Wakeman, Rick/David Bowie, "Space Oddity" (1969)

Additional players
Patrick Warren (Amy Mann, Michael Penn)

EAR WITNESS
Like listening to a fish play the saxophone. An unreal, other-worldly, ethereal, and utterly engrossing sonic treat.

WURLITZER ELECTRIC PIANO

COMMON NAME
Wurlitzer Electric Piano

FULL NAME
Wurlitzer EP 200 Electromechanical
Stringless Piano

ALIAS
Wurly

YEAR OF ORIGN
1955

PLACE OF ORIGIN
Corinth, Mississippi

SONIC SOURCE
Hammer strikes corresponding metal reed upon depression of key. The resulting vibration converted to an electric signal via a surrounding electrostatic pickup plate. Release of key triggers damper mechanism.

Wurlitzer EP 200 Electromechanical Stringless Piano

DESCRIPTION
Plastic body (usually black), 56 lbs. without legs or pedal.

CONTROLS
Power/Volume

Tremolo (fixed rate, adjustable depth)

TUNING
Solder added to end of corresponding reed adds mass, slowing down the vibration rate and thus lowering pitch. Ideally the integrity of solder shape is maintained to preserve the instrument's overall timbre. Reeds are notorious for easy breakage.

Speakers amplified internally. Optional mono output to external amplifier.

BACKGROUND
Benjamin F. Miessner, who during the early 1930s invented the Electromechanical Piano (consisting of one pickup for each string), leased the related patents to the Everett Piano Company who introduced the Everett Orgatron, an electric organ that blew air over reeds placed near electrostatic pickups.

Wurlitzer followed by incorporating these same principles in the design of their instrument, releasing their first early model in 1955. Production ceased in 1982.

ACCOMPLICES
Crumar: RP-29; Roady; Roadrunner
Hohner: Pianet
Korg: SV-1
Nord: Electro 2; EX

KEY PLAYERS

WURLITZER

Charles, Ray, "What'd I Say" (1959)
Davies, Rick/Supertramp, "Bloody Well Right" (1974)
Deacon, John/Queen, "You're My Best Friend" (1975)
Fagan, Donald/Steely Dan, "Do It Again" (1972)
Greenspoon, Jimmy/Three Dog Night, "Mama Told Me Not to Come" (1970)
Greenspoon, Jimmy/Three Dog Night, "Joy to the World" (1971)
Lamm, Robert/Chicago, "Feelin' Stronger Every Day" (1973)
Mannassa, Rick/Bob Seger and the Silver Bullet Band, "Turn the Page" (1972)
McLagen, Ian/The Faces, "Stay with Me" (1971)
McLagen, Ian/The Rolling Stones, "Miss You" (1978)
Oldham, Spooner/Aretha Franklin, "I Never Loved a Man (The Way I Love You)" (1967)
Rolie, Gregg/Santana, "Black Magic Woman" (1970)
Tench, Benmont/Tom Petty and the Heartbreakers, "Breakdown" (1977)
Wright, Richard/Pink Floyd, "Money" (1973)
Zawinul, Joe/Julian "Cannonball" Adderley, "Mercy Mercy Mercy" (1966)

HOHNER

Argent, Rod/The Zombies, "She's Not There" (1964)
Cummings, Burton/The Guess Who, "These Eyes" (1968)
Gallucci, Don/The Kingsmen, "Louie Louie" (1963)
Greenspoon, Jimmy/Three Dog Night, "Joy to the World" (1971)
Jones, John Paul/Led Zeppelin, "Misty Mountain Hop" (1971)
Jones, John Paul/Led Zeppelin, "No Quarter" (1973)
Yester, Jerry/The Lovin' Spoonful, "Summer in the City" (1966)

EAR WITNESS

It will rock you on a plane
It will rock you on a train
It will rock you on the street
It will rock you to your feet

When you play it in your sweater
You will know there's nothing better
For a fiercely furious sound
A finer keyboard can't be found.

FENDER RHODES ELECTRIC PIANO

COMMON NAME
Rhodes

FULL NAME
Fender Rhodes Electric Piano

YEAR OF ORIGIN
1946

PLACE OF MANUFACTURE
Fullerton, California

SONIC SOURCE
Depression of key activates hammer while simultaneously lifting damper from metal tine. Hammer strikes tine, inducing signal; surrounding magnetic pickups facilitate electronic transduction. Dampers cease vibration upon release of key.

Rhodes Mark II Stage 73 Piano

Photo by Aslak Raanes; Trondheim, Norway

DESCRIPTION
Models:
Stage 73
Suitcase 73
Stage 88
Suitcase 88

Stage models require external amplification and speakers. Mono 1/4" out, no power supply required.

Suitcase models carry internal amp and speakers in separate assembly, stereo vibrato with variable depth and rate controls, tone controls. Stereo 1/4" outs.

Model number refers to number of keys.

Notes are tuned by sliding a small spring across each tine; pitch is raised as spring approaches fulcrum.

Tone can be customized via readjustment of hammers and pickups.

BACKGROUND
Harold Rhodes (1910–2000), an acclaimed piano teacher and former serviceman in the Army Air Corps, invented the instrument as a morale booster for injured soldiers. The original prototype was made from spare aircraft parts and named the "Army Air Corps Piano."

Rhodes founded the Rhodes Piano Corporation in 1946. It was acquired by Fender in 1965. Fender Rhodes' first collaborative effort was the 32-note PianoBass, made famous by Ray Manzarek of The Doors.

Fender Rhodes ceased production in 1984.

ACCOMPLICES
Korg: SV-1
Nord: Electro 2, EX
RMI: Electra-Piano
Roland: Fantom X-6

KEY PLAYERS

RHODES

Creme, Lol/10cc, "I'm Not in Love" (1975)
Corea, Chick, "Spain" (1971)
Cutler-Lewis, David/Ambrosia, "Biggest Part of Me" (1980)
Duke, George/Frank Zappa, "Dirty Love" (1973)
Fagan, Donald, "New Frontier" (1982)
Feldman, Victor/Steely Dan, "Hey 19" (1980) (author's favorite Rhodes solo)
Gonsky, Lawrence/Looking Glass, "Brandy (You're a Fine Girl)" (1972)
Griffin, Paul/Steely Dan, "Peg" (1977)
Hancock, Herbie, "Chameleon" (1973)
Joel, Billy, "Just the Way You Are" (1977)
John, Elton, "Daniel" (1973)
Konte, Frank "Skip"/Blues Image, "Ride Captain Ride" (1970)
Lamm, Robert/Chicago, "Feelin' Stronger Everyday" (1973)
Lorber, Jeff/Jeff Lorber Fusion, "Lights Out" (1979)
Manzarek, Ray/The Doors, "Riders on the Storm (1971)
Mayo, Bob/Peter Frampton, "Baby, I Love Your Way" (1976)
McDonald, Michael/The Doobie Brothers, "Minute by Minute" (1978)
Preston, Billy/The Beatles, "Get Back" (1969)
Sample, Joe/The Crusaders, "Street Life" (1979)
Sting/The Police, "Spirits in the Material World" (1981)
Stone, Sly/Sly & The Family Stone, "Family Affair" (1971)
Wonder, Stevie, "You Are the Sunshine of My Life" (1973)
Woolfson, Eric/Alan Parsons Project, "I Wouldn't Want to Be Like You" (1977)
Wright, Richard/Pink Floyd, "Time" (1973)
Young, Larry/Miles Davis, "Pharaoh's Dance" (1969)
Zawinul, Joe/Weather Report, "Birdland" (1977)

RMI

Phillinganes, Greg/Stevie Wonder, "Isn't She Lovely" (1976)

EAR WITNESS

The belle of the ball, the cream in your musical coffee, sweet and sour together forever. Great for appetizers OR main course. Goes well with everything.

HOHNER CLAVINET

COMMON NAME
Clavinet

FULL NAME
Hohner Clavinet Electromechanical
Keyboard Instrument

ALIAS
Model C, D6, E7

A.K.A.
Clav

Hohner Clavinet C

YEAR OF ORIGN
1964

PLACE OF ORIGIN
Trossingen, Germany

SONIC SOURCE
Depression of key impinges metal, rubber-tipped anvil upon individually tuned string. Hammer-on style of keystroke makes aftertouch control possible. Signal transduction induced through series of magnetic single-coil bar pickups placed above and below strings, controlled via six rocker-type switches. Yarn damper system ceases vibration of string upon release of key.

DESCRIPTION
Five octaves (60 keys), 68.35 lbs. Mono output. D6 requires 9-volt battery.
Screw adjustment alters tension of strings for tuning.
Works well with Wah pedal, Phase shifter, and Chorus.

BACKGROUND
Invented by Ernst Zacharias, a staff engineer for Hohner, who is also credited with the Hohner Pianet. The most popular model, the D6, was introduced in 1971. Production ceased in 1982.

ACCOMPLICES
Hohner Accordion: bellows-driven free-reed keyboard instrument.
Hohner Melodica: wind-driven free-reed keyboard instrument.

KEY PLAYERS
Casey, Harry Wayne/KC and the Sunshine Band, "That's the Way" (1975)
Dragon, Daryl/Captain & Tennille, "Love Will Keep Us Together" (1975)
Grace, Rocke/Joe Walsh, "Rocky Mountain Way" (1973)
Grolnick, Don/Steely Dan, "Black Cow" (1977)
Hudson, Garth/The Band, "Up on Cripple Creek" (1969)
Jones, John Paul/Led Zeppelin, "Trampled Underfoot" (1975)
McDonald, Michael/The Doobie Brothers, "It Keeps You Runnin'" (1976)
McVie, Christine/Fleetwood Mac, "You Make Loving Fun" (1977)
Middleton, Max/The Jeff Beck Group, "Max's Tune" (1971)
Murphy, Kevin/Rufus featuring Chaka Khan, "Tell Me Something Good" (1974)
Preston, Billy, "Outa-Space" (1971)
Preston, Billy/The Rolling Stones, "Doo Doo Doo Doo (Heartbreaker)" (1973)
Tandy, Richard/Electric Light Orchestra, "Evil Woman" (1975)
Wonder, Stevie, "Superstition" (1972)

EAR WITNESS
You will never find a more bustling hive of funky hustle.

ELECTRONIC SONIC SYNTHESIZER

COMMON NAME
Synthesizer

FULL NAME
Electronic Sonic Synthesizer

ALIAS
Synth

YEAR OF ORIGN
1964

PLACE OF ORIGIN
New York, New York

Minimoog Model D

SONIC SOURCE

This instrument incorporates electrical currents moving in a circuit (oscillator) to simulate the vibrations that form sound. Each note of the keyboard triggers a different voltage, usually by a factor of one volt per octave. It may be monophonic or polyphonic, and can incorporate analog and/or digital technology, depending on the make and model.

Types of sonic synthesis include:

- Additive Synthesis: sound is built up from a series of sine ways of varying frequencies and amplitudes.

- Frequency Modulation Synthesis (FM Synthesis): sound generated through combination of like waveforms resulting in a more complex waveform possessing highly intricate harmonic characteristics.

- Granular Synthesis: sound generated through combination of digital microsamples (1 to 50 milliseconds in length).

- Physical Modeling Synthesis: sound formed via incorporation of mathematical algorithms designed to emulate instruments and spaces.

- Sample-based Synthesis: tones generated from direct sampling, manipulation, and editing of existing sounds and instruments.

- Subtractive Synthesis: a tone rich in harmonics is produced, the unwanted frequencies are then filtered out.

- Wavetable Synthesis: sound generated though combinations of multiple, single cycle waveforms.

DESCRIPTION
Controls:

VCO (voltage controlled oscillator(s): generates pitch, sets waveform type (i.e., sawtooth, square, sine, pulse, etc.).

VCF (voltage controlled filter): determines tone via high pass, low pass, frequency boost/cut, resonance, etc.

VCA (voltage controlled amplifier): sets volume and generates envelope of tone via attack/sustain/decay/release controls.

LFO (low frequency oscillator): generates lower frequencies inducing vibrato and other modulation effects.

Other performance features may include a white noise generator, portamento, pitch bend, frequency modulation, touch sensitivity, and aftertouch, as well as programmable presets.

An Arpeggiator is a sequencer that automatically cycles through a set series of triggered notes.

Various combinations of wheels, joysticks, knobs, sliders, and buttons are incorporated to manipulate these functions.

MIDI (Musical Instrument Digital Interface):

Dave Smith, currently of Dave Smith Instruments and founder of Sequential Circuits, coined the acronym in 1981.

A synth PAD refers to one or more sustained notes held throughout a musical passage, usually for the purposes of establishing atmosphere and/or providing sonic support.

A synth PATCH refers to a specific, generated sound; patchchords were formerly required to accomplish this endeavor.

BACKGROUND

Dr. Robert Arthur Moog (1934–2005), a former Theremin manufacturer and dealer, fostered his initial ideas on sound synthesis in 1964 at Columbia University in New York. His work was preceded by Elisha Gray, who invented the synthesizer in 1876, as well as Harry Olsen, who in 1954 developed the RCA Music Synthesizer. His initial offering, the first commercially available synthesizer ever produced, was the modular 900 series, released in 1967.

The Minimoog, one of Moog's more popular later models, was produced from 1971 to 1981.

The Prophet 5, the first programmable polyphonic synth, was introduced by Sequential Circuits in 1977.

ACCOMPLICES

ARP: 2600; Chroma; Odyssey; Pro Soloist; String Ensemble; et al.

CASIO: CZ series; FZ series; VL series; VZ series; various portables

EMU: Emulator; et al.

ENSONIQ: Mirage; et al.

EMS: VCS3; et al.

FAIRLIGHT: CMI (Computer Musical Instrument)

KORG: Mono/Poly; PolySix; Poly-800; Karma; Triton; et al.; various clones.

MOOG: early modular synthesizers; Minimoog; Taurus (bass pedals); Micromoog; Moogerfooger; Little Phatty; Prodigy; Rogue; et al.

NEW ENGLAND DIGITAL: Synclavier

NORD: Lead 2x

OBERHEIM: Matrix series; OBX; Voice series; et al.

ROLAND: D-50; Jupiter series; JX series; Juno series; System 100 series; et al.

SEQUENTIAL CIRCUITS: Prophet 5; et al.

YAMAHA: CS-80; DX7; SK series; Motif series; et al.; various clones and portables

KEY PLAYERS

ARP
Banks, Tony/Genesis, "Cinema Show" (1973)
Hancock, Herbie, "Chameleon" (1973)
Townsend, Pete/The Who, "Who are You" (1978)
Winter, Edgar, "Frankenstein" (1973)
Wright, Gary, "Dream Weaver" (1975)

EMS
Townsend, Pete/The Who, "Won't Get Fooled Again" (1971)
Wright, Richard/Pink Floyd, "On the Run" (1973)

ENSONIQ
Jam, Jimmy/Janet Jackson, "Control" (1986)
Wallinger, Karl/World Party, "Ship of Fools" (1986)

EMU
Hardcastle, Paul, "19" (1985)
Gabriel, Peter, "Sledgehammer" (1986)

FAIRLIGHT
Fast, Larry/Peter Gabriel, "Shock the Monkey" (1982)

KORG
Michaeli, Mic/Europe, "The Final Countdown (1986)

MOOG
Emerson, Keith/Emerson, Lake & Palmer, "Lucky Man" (1970)
Harrison, George/The Beatles, "Here Comes the Sun" (1969)
Numan, Gary, "Cars" (1979)
Tomita, Isao, "The Planets" (1977)
Wonder, Stevie, "Boogie On Reggae Woman" (1974)
Worrell, Bernie/Parliament-Funkadelic, "Flashlight" (1978)
Wright, Gary, "Dream Weaver" (1975)
Wright, Richard/Pink Floyd, "Shine On You Crazy Diamond" (1974)
(also see Brian Kehew and Roger Joseph Manning Jr./The Moog Cookbook)

NEW ENGLAND DIGITAL
Banks, Tony/Genesis, "That's All" (1983)
Coppola, Tom/Paul Simon, "Think Too Much" (1983)
Pocaro, Steve/Michael Jackson, "Thriller" (1982)

OBERHEIM
Lee, Geddy/Rush, "Limelight" (1981)
Van Halen, Eddie/Van Halen, "Jump!" (1984)

ROLAND
Cain, Jonathan/Journey, "Separate Ways" (1983)
Jam, Jimmy/Human League, "Human" (1986)
Rhodes, Nick/Duran Duran, "Rio" (1982)

SEQUENTIAL CIRCUITS
Badarou, Wally/Grace Jones, "Pull Up to the Bumper" (1981)
Cuomo, Bill/Kim Karnes, "Bette Davis Eyes" (1981)
McCartney, Paul, "Wonderful Christmastime" (1979)

YAMAHA
Faltermeyer, Harlold, "Axel F" (1984)
Hammer, Jan, "Miami Vice Theme" (1984)
Paich, David/Toto, "Africa" (1982)
Pleasure, Morris/Michael Jackson, "Wanna Be Startin' Somethin'" (1983)
Townsend, Pete/The Who, "Eminence Front" (1982)

EAR WITNESS

"There is nothing more contrived than a box with holes in it the shape of an 'f,' with maple on one side, spruce on the other... Electronics is as natural as wood or metal working. There's no reason why an electronic instrument cannot be every bit as expressive and appealing as a traditional acoustic instrument."

−Robert Moog

"In fact, the synthesizers I use are very, very simple indeed... The synthesizers I own are the most modest synthesizers you can get."

−Brian Eno, 1978

Synthesizers were previously designed to emulate real instruments, as well as to create original sounds. Sampling technology, however, has made the former half of this effort obsolete. Like the rest of us in the music business, their power today lies in their ability to generate unique, individual sounds that simply cannot be created through any other means.

KEY BASICS

"Before starting the car, I know where I'm going."
—**Thich Nhat Hanh,** *Being Peace*

OK, admit it. You've coveted your neighbor's guitar. Don't be ashamed, we've all done it. Who wouldn't want a piece of that action? Shredding those wicked arpeggios out in the open where everyone can see them, moving around the stage like an over-caffeinated hamster, feeding back and making those wicked cruncha-cruncha sounds. At some point a keyboard player's gotta shrug his or her shoulders and think, "How can I compete with that?"

Well, I've got bad news and good news. The bad news is that keyboards will never magically become guitars—and I don't care how many Keytars you show me, them things just ain't natural. The good news is that the keyboards have a beautiful, magical, irrefutable cool all their own. They are vital in two ways: they serve as both the musical glue that effectively blends all of the different sounding sonorities together, AND the special sauce that adds that perfect sonic kick to the overall sound. In baker's terms, they are both the flour that binds the cake AND the icing that makes it ultimately irresistible. They are the band's sonic facilitator.

KEY THEORY
Like evolution you can dance to.

INTERVALS
Yeah they're so spaced out.

An interval is the distance between two tones. Here they are, along with some songs whose first two notes use the given interval

     minor 2nd – Theme from *Jaws*

     major 2nd – Frère Jacques

     minor 3rd – What Child Is This?; Smoke on the Water (Deep Purple)

     major 3rd – Morning Has Broken; Blister in the Sun (Violent Femmes)

     perfect 4th – Amazing Grace; Here Comes the Bride

     tritone (augmented 4th/diminished 5th) – Maria (*West Side Story*)

     perfect 5th – Twinkle, Twinkle, Little Star; Scarborough Fair

     minor 6th – Because (The Beatles)

     major 6th – My Bonnie Lies Over the Ocean; NBC Theme

     minor 7th – Theme from *Star Trek*; There's a Place for Us

     major 7th – *Fantasy Island* Theme

     octave – Over the Rainbow

Here's what they look like written out:

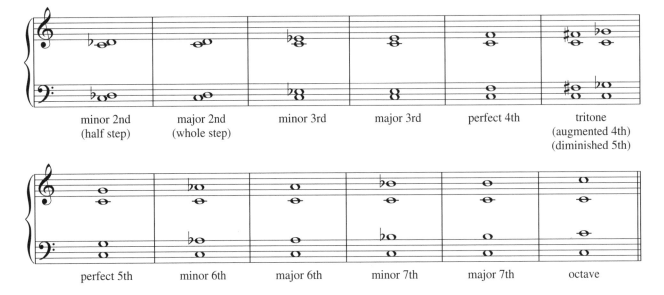

KEY SIGNATURES

Sharp cheddar and flat champagne.

Here are all the keys, along with their corresponding sharps or flats. This is known as the "key signature." You'll notice there's a constant companion minor key for every major one; this is known as the "relative minor." A major key and its relative minor share the same key signature and are always separated by a minor third.

SCALES

You want them to want you.

Practice makes perfect. There's absolutely no substitute for these babies: they make the whole world sing. Here are the major, minor, blues, and chromatic scales. Once you master them, you've pretty much got it covered.

I generally run each scale starting with straight eighth notes, progress to eighth-note triplets, and finally to sixteenths. As my familiarity increases, I gradually speed up the tempo of the exercise.

As you practice, be sure to keep your wrists, hands, and fingers as relaxed as possible. Ideally you should feel no stress or tension; all the energy should be flowing outward, toward the keys. Play each note carefully and deliberately, using only the minimal musculature required to strike each individual key. Let your fingers arch naturally.

I recommend beginning your sequence extremely slowly, focusing on correct fingering and precise, accurate keystrokes. Make sure you're striking each note using only the muscles specifically related to the incorporated finger. Then push yourself; start again, in every key, at a pace just slightly beyond where you feel comfortable. Over time, this deliberate means of practice will lead to mastery.

MAJOR SCALES

The happiest scales of all.

This the one everyone starts with. The major is the most basic and fundamental of all the scales. C major has no sharps or flats. What could be simpler?

Scale Degrees (also applies to minor)

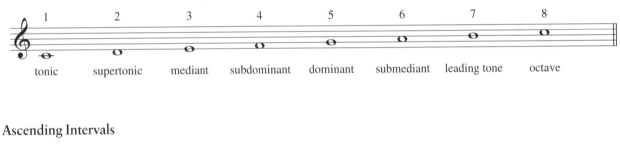

Ascending Intervals

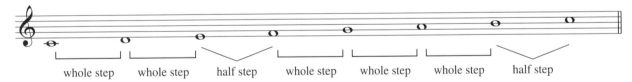

Here are all 12 major scales, with the appropriate fingerings:

Cue up Track 1 on the CD and listen to this exercise example in E major.

MINOR SCALES

The scales that make you cry.

For each and every major scale there is a corresponding minor scale referred to as its "relative minor," so named because it shares the same key signature. A major scale's relative minor can always be determined by going down a minor third, or three half steps. For example, the relative minor of C major is A minor.

Ascending Intervals

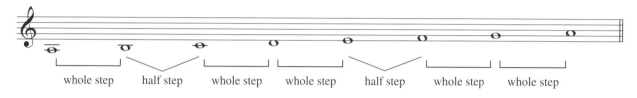

Here are all 12 minor scales, with the appropriate fingerings:

Go to Track 2 on the CD and listen to this exercise example in C♯ minor.

BLUES SCALES

Don't leave home without them.

Fundamental to blues, rock, R&B, and most other forms of popular music, the blues scales consist of six notes (hexatonic) and are the gateway to modern musical improvisation. Once you get these scales down, you will be able to jam with anybody in any key. Period.

Ascending Intervals

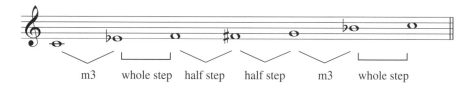

Here are all 12 blues scales, with the appropriate fingerings:

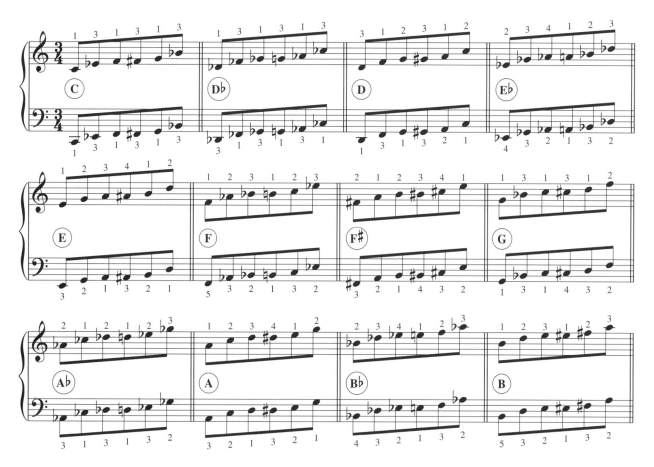

Track 3 on the CD features the E blues scale. Give it a listen.

CHROMATIC SCALES

Every note, every time.

"Chroma" is the Greek word for color; the derivative term "chromatic" is thusly applied, as the scale covers all of the named notes—at least according to Western notation. The chromatic scales consist entirely of half steps, in consecutive order.

On a keyboard, chromatic scales use every key, black and white. In music notation the ascending chromatic scale uses sharp signs, while the descending chromatic scale uses flat signs

The ascending chromatic scale starting on C:

The descending chromatic scale starting on C:

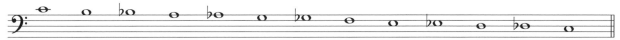

Here are all 12 chromatic scales, with the appropriate fingerings:

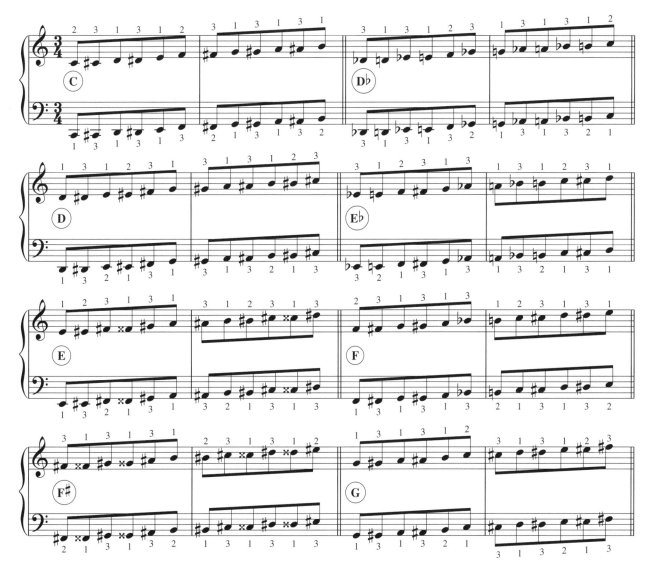

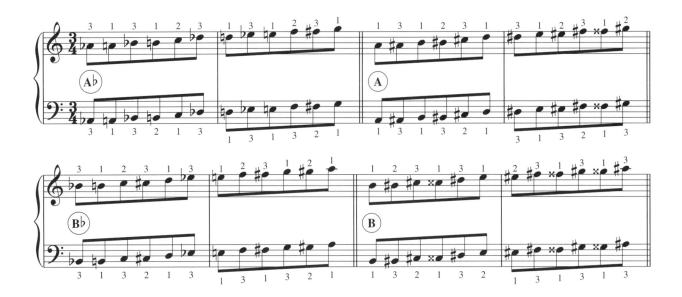

Cue up Track 4 on the CD and listen to this exercixe example of the C♯ chromatic scale.

SEVEN COMMON CHORDS

and a Farfisa in a pear tree.

Here are seven frequently heard chords, along with their matching notation and written abbreviations. A diminished chord is composed entirely of minor thirds, and an augmented chord is made up of only major thirds.

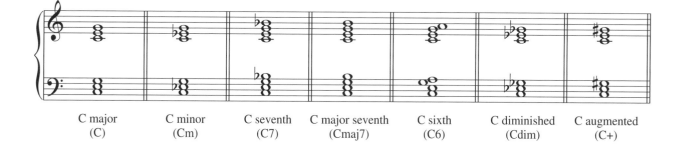

C major	C minor	C seventh	C major seventh	C sixth	C diminished	C augmented
(C)	(Cm)	(C7)	(Cmaj7)	(C6)	(Cdim)	(C+)

CHORD INVERSIONS

I love you just they way you were.

You can take any chord—in this case, a C7—and flip it around, causing it to sound differently and generate different moods. Picking which inversion to use generally depends on which combination of notes most effectively serves the song.

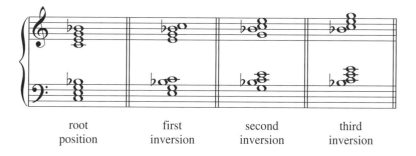

root position	first inversion	second inversion	third inversion

TWO MORE FOR THE ROAD
Triads and Dominant Sevenths

Here are the major, minor, diminished, and augmented triads, along with some extremely dominant 7ths (seventh chord based on fifth note of diatonic scale). They can be run in the same manner as the scales. Once you master them in root position, try flipping them around, beginning with the third (first inversion) and proceeding with the fifth (second inversion).

TRIADS

DOMINANT SEVENTHS

Play in root position, then in first, second, and third inversions.

KEY STARTS

Inversions, comps, and fills.

INVERSION AVERSION THERAPY

It happens to everyone: you see a G major chord and you play it all nice and straight; root first, with a cute little third in the middle and pointy-pointy perfect fifth of a top. Neat and tidy, right? Wrong! You've got to move those puppies around, make 'em dance! Inversions make a vanilla chord into a nasty and beguiling hot fudge sundae!

The keyboardist's chordal inversion strategy must include a reaction to the sonic space surrounding him/her. At its best, it functions as a harmonic barometer, actively filling in spaces while simultaneously ensuring that the musical milkshake is not too thick to drink through a straw.

How do you know which position to use? Well, like many things in life, it totally depends. Questions I often ask myself include:

- Which sonorities are already covered by the other instruments?

- Which range best serves the fullness of the overall sound?

- Which chord choices will best make the other players' choices sound better?

- How can my musical meanderings best serve the song?

CD Track 5

Check out Track 5 on the CD for an example of what I mean:

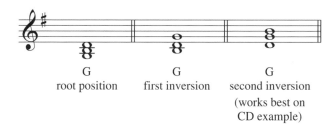

G	G	G
root position	first inversion	second inversion (works best on CD example)

COMPING

Mama said back you up.

What is comping? Short for "accompanying," basically it's making an effective, vital musical contribution to an existing set of repeated chords. Like a rhythm guitarist, a keyboard player can add a minimal yet essential part to any set of changes. Whether supporting a solo, contributing to a groove, or providing a complementary sonic texture underneath a lead vocal, comping is an integral and extremely effective musical tool for any player. By utilizing the right voicings, color, and space, the parts you choose can literally pull a tune over the edge in just the right way—or, conversely, drag it into the soulless pit of a grooveless netherworld. As the instrument with the final say, it's the keyboardist's mission to discover and add that perfect seasoning to the overall musical meal. If the song is a hot dog, consider yourself the spicy mustard.

For me, good comping all comes down to the three R's: reactive, rhythmic, repetition.

- Reactive: What are the other parts being played? What parts of the sonic spectrum aren't being covered? Where are the spaces between the notes?

- Rhythmic: How can my part add to the groove? What combination of notes and spaces can I lay down that will provide the most support, and not get in the way?

- Repetition: By finding my part and sticking with it, my fellow musicians will have a safe and steady sonic support system upon which to build.

Of course, underlying all these choices is the ultimate desire to serve the song. As keyboard players, it's our prerogative to remove our individual selves from the picture and completely surrender to the music. This is our credo, an essential element crucial to the process of procuring the perfect part.

I've included three examples of comping on the accompanying CD. Each is notated and discussed on the following pages.

FUNK

Instrument: Organ
Key: F major

L.H. ad lib.

In this example I'm playing an organ part to complement the rhythm guitar. The bass is providing the dynamic movement, the drums are furnishing the foundation. I'm doing my best to lay back and groove while trying not to step on anybody's toes. My right hand is playing the chords while my left hand is providing percussive accents, a common organ-playing technique. I'm playing an Fmaj9, but not including the root, as the guitar has that covered with his Fmaj7. I'm also raising the chord up a half-step every eight counts to provide some fun tension, and I'm changing up the pattern slightly for color. This type of interlocking structure can prove to be extremely effective and engaging, especially within the funk idiom.

BLUES

Instrument: Piano
Key: G major

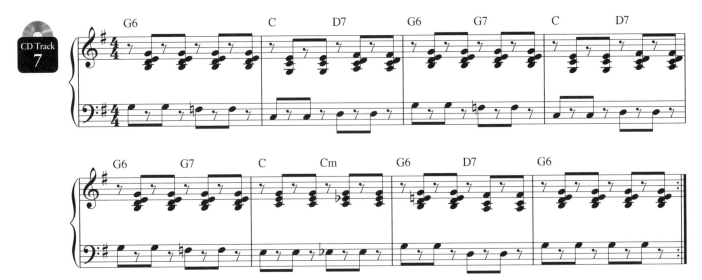

I'm playing off-beats with my right hand while doubling the bass line with my left. I often find doubling the bass line to be very satisfying, especially on an upright. Nothing fancy, just keeping everything regular and steady. I'm trying to match the shuffle the drummer's playing, emphasizing the swung "and" of 1 opposite the bass and acoustic guitar. I'm also adding a 6th to the G major chord to give it that old-timey, classic feel. A singer or instrumentalist could easily vamp over this, as is often the case with blues. Simple and effective.

ROCK

Instrument: Clavinet
Key: G minor

Straight-ahead groove, guitar and bass are doubling the main line, screaming lead guitar. What's a keyboard player to do? Bring something new to the table. The clavinet via an auto-wah effect has a nice sassy appeal, and the midrange tonality works well between the well-covered highs and lows. I'm playing a rhythmic comp with an engaging melodic hook, once again using my left hand purely as a percussive foil. Ideally, I've found an uncovered sonic space within which I've provided an additional latch for both the band and the audience via repetition of a simple yet supportive musical phrase.

That's what good comping is all about.

FILLS

Don't top the tank!

Living somewhere between solos and comping, fills are the musical bread crumbs of the business, the pearls we throw down to support the groove and/or just prove to everyone that we're listening hard.

And they're so darn fun! I bet you want to do them all the time! Because they're flashy and cool and just so darn fun fun fun!

Until you crash. And then it's tough. Because nobody will want to play with you anymore. Because everyone wants a turn. Don't Bogart that fill, my friend. Pass it along to G.

Like a fine wine, a good fill lifts the spirit without drawing attention to itself. It slips by without anyone noticing. It makes the ice sparkle without freezing the glass. If used sparingly and with care, fills can serve both the intent and character of the music being played, as well as your ever-present and incurable case of guitar envy.

Here are two examples to show you what I mean. Roll that classic bean footage!

ACOUSTIC ROCK

Instrument: Organ
Key: E major

One way to execute a good fill is to repeat a strong, catchy motif that functions as a passive hook while providing counterpoint and sonic balance. For the first few bars, I'm stretching out, filling up space without drawing too much attention. Then I go to the motif.

FUNK

Instrument: Organ

Key: D minor

Part of the art of the good fill involves knowing when to step back. In this example, I set up a motif for the groove, then fill around the vocal, endeavoring to support the singer and maintain the excitement of the track.

KEY APPLICATIONS

I play it, you slay it.

This "call and response" section of the book—in other words, the fun part—consists of 31 examples, grouped by genre (Blues, Country, Jazz, Latin, R&B, Rock, and World). All are played on the CD, as well as notated and explained in the book. The second half of each track features the accompanying band alone, leaving space for you to try the parts yourself, or make up new ones.

Don't be frustrated if you don't get it right the first time. Deconstruct the phrases, slow them down, and repeat them until you don't have to think about them. With patience and persistence, the music will become a part of you.

OK, ready? Great! Let's jam!

BLUES

12 bars, no waiting.

MINOR BLUES

Instrument: Wurlitzer Electric Piano

Key: F minor

Keytext: This is a classic minor blues run in the vein B.B. King's "The Thrill Is Gone." Moderate tempo, nothing flashy, good solid groove. Relax into it.

M.O.*: The role of the keys here is to support and fill. I'm playing off the guitar hits and keeping things simple and in the pocket, supporting a potential vocalist or solo. A light touch on the comping keeps the part from becoming too heavy.

Left hand: Sparse lower octaves, light runs with right hand.

Right hand: Midrange seventh chords, light runs to fill.

Hot hint: Tremolo on Wurlitzer gives the part an overall funky feel.

*For those needing a quick refresher course in Latin, M.O. is short for *modus operandi*, a method of operating or functioning.

BLUES SHUFFLE

Instrument: Piano
Key: G major

Keytext: The blues shuffle is one of the most basic and satisfying of forms, endlessly engaging and wickedly wondrous. It offers the opportunity to say a lot by saying a little. Even the simplest of parts and solos can sound totally legitimate and "real" if played with conviction.

M.O.: Piano is playing that classic minor third triplet fill we've all heard so many times before, and for good reason: it works. Laid back, not in a hurry. Dancing around the structure while endeavoring not to be intrusive. By staying out of the way of the mid and lower tones, this simple-yet-effective riff repletion works by carving out its own sonic niche in the higher register.

Left hand: Reaching for can of orange juice.

Right hand: Loose wrists, relaxed fingers, minimal movement. Occasional glissando added for color.

Hot hint: Once you've got this down, try soloing using the G blues scale.

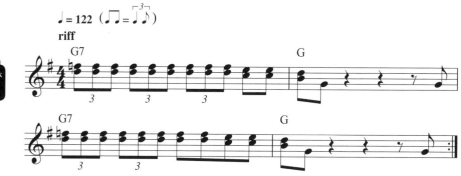

UP-TEMPO BLUES

Instrument: Piano
Key: E major

Keytext: This blues form is fast, loose, and on the prowl. Think Muddy Waters. The beat should crackle like a thousand sonic sparklers. The band gives you a two-count pickup to start.

M.O.: Piano plays minor third trills, filling up the space in a compelling, lead-like capacity. A little goes a long way here: just laying down the figures with authority and conviction can make all the difference.

Left hand: Reaching for can of tomato juice.

Right hand: Just trillin', 2nd and 4th fingers. Relax into it.

Hot hint: Utilizing the percussive aspects of the instrument provides a great base upon which to build and lock with the rhythm section. Think like a drummer.

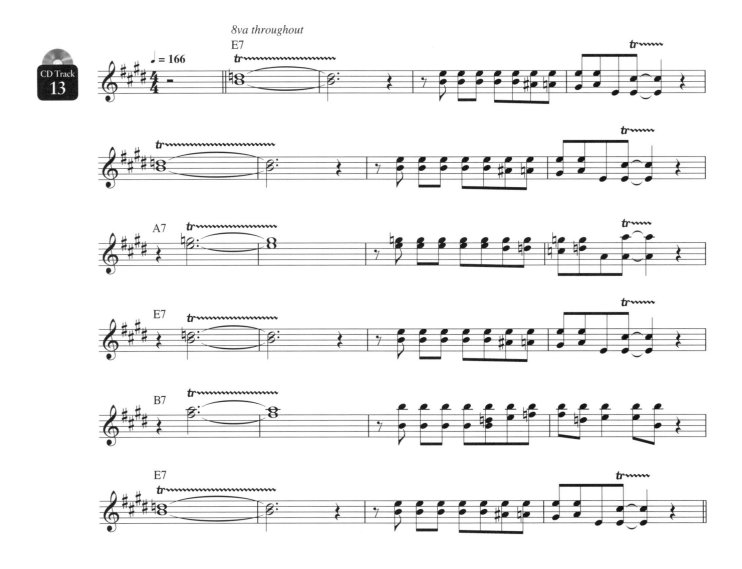

STANDARD BLUES

Instrument: Organ
Key: C major

Keytext: Nothing fancy here, just the real down low and dirty thing. Fun for hours.

M.O.: On the first pass I'm just holding down the chords, sustaining and filling over the progression while working the Leslie. Maintaining the whole notes while gradually increasing and decreasing the speed of the Leslie motor lets the organ fill things out nicely, without moving around too much. In the next pass I take a break, playing variations of the C blues scale over the changes.

Left hand: "Whooshing" up to the right hand, playing percussive off-beats.

Right hand: Unlike a piano, organ keys must remain depressed in order for the notes to sustain. This is the key difference in playing the two instruments. The right hand finds the notes, then holds them down for emphasis.

Hot hint: Excellent opportunity to exploit percussive aspects of the organ via random rhythmic note stabs (see solo).

COUNTRY
Southbound and down.

STANDARD COUNTRY

Instrument: Piano
Key: E major

Keytext: Country music is all about the words; the instruments, especially the keyboards, provide a sonic podium for the singer. A highly melodic, precise musical form.

M.O.: Adding to the overall vibe of the piece by bobbing in and out. Present, dependable riff. As common with this genre, heavy use of rapidly played transitional notes (grace notes).

Left hand: Light low octaves on the first count of every measure.

Right hand: Trill with 2nd and 3rd finger, minimal movement of wrist to support.

Hot hint: Once you get this, try soloing with the E major scale.

UP-TEMPO COUNTRY

Instrument: Piano

Key: E major

Keytext: Raucous. Barrelhouse. Honky-Tonk. These are the terms that come to mind here. Think Jerry Lee. Good-timey, dance hall feel.

M.O.: Piano is in for the party, an active participant. Lightly placed high-registered eighth notes give the piece a sparkle without being shrill.

Left hand: Aiding right hand on runs if necessary.

Right hand: Lightly played, percussive, precise. Active use of "blue notes." This run is an aggregation of the E blues scale, many variations are possible and encouraged.

Hot hint: If you learn this riff in every key, you are officially Jam Worthy!

MID-TEMPO COUNTRY

Instrument: Organ

Key: Gb major

Keytext: As the tempo slows down, so does the subject matter. We're in a more contemplative mode here, somewhere between heaven and heartbreak.

M.O.: We can create this vibe instrumentally by elongated, smoothly played passages, and light, pleasing, well-chosen parts. Glissing up to the first note, using the drawbars to select the high tone, an octave above the fundamental.

Left hand: Supporting right hand with glisses and stabs.

Right hand: As this is organ, your concentration should be more on sustaining given notes rather than overall movement.

Hot hint: Try finding midrange chords to sustain along with the acoustic guitar. This is another option for a compelling comp.

ROADHOUSE COUNTRY

Instrument: Piano

Key: D major

Keytext: "The piano has been drinking." —Tom Waits

M.O.: In this example, I offer two different starts. The first is a classic blues riff, which I play over the changes twice. Notice the notes are "rolled," or played rapidly back and forth. After that, I play a set of chords that act as a fill, while staying out of the way of the guitar. I play that twice, then there's space for you to try it.

Left hand: Light lower octaves.

Right hand: Loose as a goose. Fluid, like your libation.

Hot hint: Referencing personal tragedy while performing this style of music is highly recommended.

JAZZ
The swing thing.

STRAIGHT-AHEAD JAZZ

Instrument: Piano
Key: G major

Keytext: Jazz is the land of syncopation and freedom. It's like an ocean: the deeper it goes, the farther out you want to swim. With its intricate voicings and clever resolutions, it serves as musical manna for the most sophisticated of aural palates.

M.O: I'm following a set of basic changes and just letting it rip. As the cut is in G major, I'm simply incorporating the notes of the G major scale: upward and downward arpeggios, rapid runs, rhythmic stabs, rapid glisses. Having fun.

Left hand: In jazz, the left hand frequently functions as the rhythm guitar of the band, playing inversions and off-beats, leaving the right hand free and assisting it when necessary.

Right hand: Working the G major scale.

Hot hint: Start simply: it's not about the number of notes you play, but the intent with which you play them. Stretch out with your solo, let the groove move you.

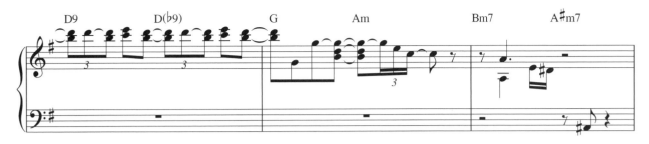

FUSION

Instrument: Fender Rhodes Electric Piano

Key: B minor

Keytext: Fusion is a cross-pollination of jazz and rock. The genre incorporates the sophisticated voicings of the former while enthusiastically utilizing the electric instrumentation and subsequent big sound of the latter.

M.O.: The electric piano is an extremely common instrument in fusion, as it offers the harmonic complexities of an acoustic piano while reaping the amplified benefits of an electric axe.

Left hand: As with the previous piece, the left hand incorporates the qualities of a rhythm guitar, playing the B minor and E major inversions underneath the right hand.

Right hand: Playing the riff. Fingers, hand, and wrist are relaxed. Minimal movement.

Hot hint: Fun to solo over with B minor blues scale.

LOUNGE JAZZ

Instrument: Piano

Key: D major

Keytext: You're in the lounge of a groovy downtown hotel, and the band is swinging. The music is light and airy, mildly compelling, but not intrusive.

M.O.: The piano tinkles like ice in a glass. I play the groove twice, then you hit it. Watch for the ritardando (gradual slowing) at the end of the piece.

Left hand: Playing chordal lead line in tandem with right hand.

Right hand: Playing chordal lead line in tandem with left hand, glissing downward when appropriate.

Hot hint: Initiate tip jar action by putting in a couple of bucks to give people the hint.

SMOOTH JAZZ

Instrument: Electric Piano
Key: E minor

Keytext: You hear it in the cab on the way to the airport. You hear it at the mall when you're buying some jeans. You hear it in the waiting room at your dentist's office. Like it or lump it, smooth jazz is everywhere.

M.O.: Keyboards are generally highly prevalent in this genre—because they're so smooth! In this example, the band plays the changes while I play two examples of fills. Eight bars separate each example so you can try them both.

Left hand: Lower octaves play supporting root of chords.

Right hand: Working in tandem with the sustain pedal.

Hot hint: Once you get the gist of these, try improvising your own fills over the progression.

LATIN

I want to Latin America!

STANDARD LATIN

Instrument: Piano
Key: D major

Keytext: Muevete! Make your body shake!

M.O.: In Latin music, it's quite common for the piano to play a steady, repetitive ostinato over the top of a chord progression. This serves as an anchor for the band by fusing all the various melodic and rhythmic components together under the auspices of one seamless sonic foil. In this example, I play such a line four times, then the band continues for you to try it.

Left hand: Syncopated doubling of the root.

Right hand: Playing repetitive, syncopated riff. Thumb on the root, 3rd and 5th fingers on the 3rd and 5th, respectively.

Hot hint: Latin ostinatos are a riot to play and can come in many forms. Try making up your own by playing single notes within the given chord.

BOSSA

Instrument: Piano

Key: G major

Keytext: Bossa (short for bossa nova) originated in Brazil, and was popularized in large part by the work of Antonio Carlos Jobim. ("The Girl from Ipanema" is one of his best-known songs.)

M.O.: In this laid-back genre the piano frequently functions as a grand provider of melody. Here I play the lead line twice, then it's your turn.

Left hand: Single-note doubling of right hand, assisting with flourishes when needed.

Right hand: Simple, elegant presentation of melody with a modicum of flourish.

Hot hint: Try improvising your own lead line over the changes.

SAMBA

Instrument: Piano

Key: A major

Keytext: Originated in Brazil; a confluence of Brazilian and African influences.

M.O.: Once again the piano plays a lively ostinato over the changes, providing melodic and rhythmic counterpoint.

Left hand: Single-note doubling of root chord.

Right hand: Syncopated set of rhythm changes, leading off with thumb.

Hot hint: Make up your own ostinato and/or solo over the changes using the A major scale.

BEGUINE

Instrument: Piano

Key: B♭ major

Keytext: A dance originally from Martinique and widely popularized by Cole Porter's "Begin the Beguine."

M.O.: The piano plays rolling chords over the changes, mimicking the strumming of a guitar.

Left hand: Whole-note upper-octave doubling of root.

Right hand: The rolling notes have a triplet feel and lead off with the thumb. Let the rolling motion flow through your fingers, as your arm and wrist are perfectly relaxed.

Hot hint: Once you get this, try composing a lead line over the changes, much as you did with the bossa.

R&B
Rockenstern and Bluesencrantz are rad!

HIP HOP
Instrument: Synthesizer
Key: A minor

Keytext: In hip hop, the music is there primarily to serve the message and delivery of the lyrics, just as it is in country music. Hip hop is really funk stripped down to the bare essentials: a simple groove, a phat bass line, and some other light embellishment. If compelling enough, a simple eight-bar groove can be repeated ad infinitum, setting the sonic stage for the story to unfold.

M.O.: I'm playing a phat synth bass line here, slightly behind the beat of the drum machine, which adds weight to the part. The synth patch is set to scoop up or down from the note last played.

Left hand: Selectively working the joystick to add modulation to the tone.

Right hand: Playing the line lightly, carefully, and succinctly. The right hand is key with synth playing, as many of the parts require only one note at a time.

Hot hint: Bass lines are a riot. The key to a good one is to keep it simple and repetitive, only rarely adding embellishment. The line should stand on its own as compelling and complete.

FUNK

Instrument: Organ
Key: E major

Keytext: Soul meets jazz. Get up. Get into it.

M.O.: The organ is an ideal instrument for funk due to its even, laid-back demeanor. It can step out when it wants and groove in when it needs.

Left hand: Working the Leslie slow/fast control. This is sort of an intuitive move on the part of the player. When you feel the excitement build, speed things up. When you want a more relaxed feel, slow it down. The tone is like a wave, ebbing and flowing within the current of the track. Once you do this enough times, you won't even have to think about it.

Right hand: Picking out the notes and sustaining the key ones. Remember, the organ is a horse of a different color. The key to playing one well lies in the sustain, and, unlike a piano, you have no pedal upon which to rely.

Hot hint: The organ offers an infinite palate of musical colors from which to choose. Try experimenting with different tonal combinations via the drawbars or presets.

FUNK ROCK

Instrument: Clavinet

Key: G major

Keytext: It rocks but it's funky, it's funk but it rocks. It's funk rock, a fusion of funk and rock!

M.O.: The Clavinet is arguably the most percussive of the keyboard family, simply because the notes decay literally seconds after being played. Basically, with this instrument, it's all about the attack. Rhythmic accuracy and integrity are key here. Divide the groove into 16th-note subdivisions and play nimbly amongst the dancing beats.

Left hand: Playing low bass octaves and working in tandem with the right hand, holding down the groove.

Right hand: Leading the attack with offbeats and syncopated stabs. The right hand leads the process here, setting up the serve for the left hand to react to.

Hot hint: Keep your wrists nimble on both hands. Pretend you're playing a drum.

TRIP HOP

Instrument: Synthesizer

Key: C minor

Keytext: Trip hop combines aspects of hip hop and house music, then slows them down. It's a mellow, chilltastic groove.

M.O.: The synth is playing the lead line proudly, succinctly, and simply.

Left hand: Subtle working of amplitude mod with the joystick.

Right hand: Simple attacks, mild sustains, controlled releases.

Hot hint: Once you get this, try soloing using the C blues scale. Keep it simple and poignant.

MOTOWN

Instrument: Organ
Key: D minor

Keytext: Soul meets rhythm and blues. This genre is named after the world-famous record label founded in 1960 by Berry Gordy Jr.

M.O.: This is a classic Motown pattern. The snare is laying it down on every beat, not just beats 2 and 4 as usual. The guitar is echoing the snare, while the bass is holding down the pattern. The role of the organ is to glue all these parts together. To this end, I'm just holding down sustained whole notes while working the Leslie to give the part some bounce.

Left hand: Glissing up to the right hand when necessary, otherwise working the slow/fast Leslie control.

Right hand: Sustaining whole notes, minimal movement, relaxed approach.

Hot hint: Try new patterns over the groove, keeping things in the pocket, blending with the other sonorities to create a cohesive feel.

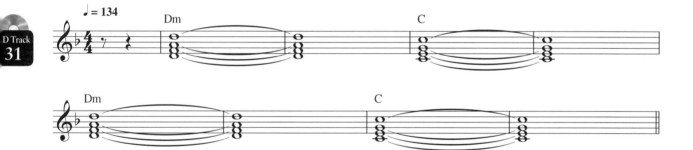

SOUL

Instrument: Electric Piano
Key: C minor

Keytext: Gospel wrapped in funk and tied up nicely with an R&B bow.

M.O.: I'm having a great time, letting it rip over the groove, soloing utilizing the C blues scale. In this example I take 16 bars, then the band continues for another 16 to give you some space to jam.

Left hand: Supporting the right hand with off-beats and underlying chordal sustains.

Right hand: Leading the charge. Fingers, hand, and wrist are relaxed, ebbing and flowing with the musical tide.

Hot hint: Soloing is not about the number of notes you play, but the choices, style, and intent with which you play them. Some of the best players out there are known for what they don't play. Start simply, and add on slowly as the spirit moves you.

ROCK

What better time than now?

HARD ROCK

Instrument: Organ
Key: D minor

Keytext: Guitars, bass, drums, keys. Rock on!

M.O.: Time to kick out some high-end organ to complement that wicked groove! I'm holding down sustained tones in the upper register, driving the piece and heightening the vibe.

Left hand: "Whooshing" up to right hand, working Leslie slow/fast control.

Right hand: Holding down targeted notes.

Hot hint: Try doubling the rhythm guitar for an extra-hard crunch!

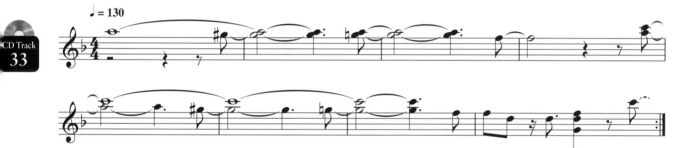

SOFT ROCK

Instrument: Wurlitzer Electric Piano
Key: D minor

Keytext: In soft rock, the instruments work together to create a low-key yet sustainable groove.

M.O.: Generally, keys have a fairly present role in this genre as they can groove without being obtrusive. In this example, I'm playing a riff over the top of the changes, keeping it simple, adding to the feel without being over the top. Note the relaxed grace-note feel coming into the G7 chord.

Left hand: Optional octave roots "on the one."

Right hand: Playing riff accurately, with intent. Relaxed fingers, hands, and wrists.

Hot hint: Try playing a mellow solo utilizing the D blues scale.

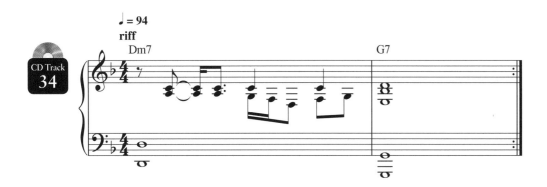

MEDIUM ROCK

Instrument: Organ
Key: G major

Keytext: This is where we live. To some degree, medium rock has played a part in your life. Not too hard to frighten Grandma, not too soft to make you sleepy. Just right in there, taking you home.

M.O.: Organ is playing signature riff, staying in the pocket, then plays example of four-bar fill.

Left hand: Glissing up to right hand, working Leslie control.

Right hand: Playing riff, sustaining targeted notes, light trills to add color.

Hot hint: Listen carefully and you can hear the click of the Leslie switch as I'm working it.

'50s ROCK

Instrument: Piano
Key: E major

Keytext: Rock was young, the audience was impressionable, and a little went a long way back then. The focus here was on simple melody and catchy lyrics.

M.O.: The piano usually echoes the part of the vocalists in this classic style. The percussive nature of the instrument aids in moving the piece along.

Left hand: Reaching for bottle of soda-pop.

Right hand: Playing chords with feeling, in time.

Hot hint: For another take, try playing the notes within the chord one-by-one, along with the electric guitar.

PARTY ROCK

Instrument: Organ
Key: C major

Keytext: This is up-tempo, good-times, no-holds-barred get-down music!

M.O.: I'm letting it all hang out with a wild, uninhibited organ solo using the C blues scale. I'm not holding back in any way. Having a blast, rocking the instrument. I highly encourage you to do the same.

Left hand: Glisses, accented off-beats playing off the right hand, working Leslie control.

Right hand: Playing solo, holding down high C, sustaining notes for emphasis. Playing grace notes and blue notes when appropriate.

Hot hint: Play the organ like a percussive instrument, take advantage of all the clicks and other crazy sounds it makes by pressing down multiple keys in quick succession.

WORLD
One is the populist number.

REGGAE
Instrument: Organ
Key: F minor

Keytext: A combination of ska and rocksteady, reggae music originated in Jamaica in the 1960s.

M.O.: In this cut, I demonstrate two staples of reggae keyboard playing, the "bubble" and the "triplet fade." The bubble consists of playing within the unused rhythmic spaces between the guitar hits, which generally fall on beats 2 and 4. This provides rhythmic counterbalance and adds an undercurrent of percolation, hence the name. The triplet fade emulates an instrument hitting a delay set to echo as triplets over a four count. In this example, I simply play the chord and slowly fade out manually with the volume fader, which produces the same result. After I demonstrate these two devices, there's space on the track for you to try them.

Left hand: Functions as the offbeat for the bubble by hitting opposite the 2 and 4 hits off the right hand. Working the volume slider.

Right hand: Hitting beats 2 and 4, along with the guitar. Playing triplet riff as left hand fades volume out.

Hot hint: Inhale.

UP-TEMPO REGGAE

Instrument: Wurlitzer Electric Piano
Key: A minor

Keytext: Speeding things up, adding a dancehall feel.

M.O.: Now that the groove is pumping, we can switch to the Wurly for some funky fills. I'm just holding down the changes and going with the flow, occupying the available midrange space underneath the guitars, providing smoothness.

Left hand: Sparse offbeats off right hand added for color.

Right hand: Holding out sustained notes, occasional fills. Relaxed, minimal movement.

Hot hint: Start adding to the fill, work up your own groove. There are many ways to make this happen, both rhythmically and melodically. Be creative, don't censor.

INTERNATIONAL

Instrument: Synthesizer
Key: G minor

Keytext: The sort of groove you might hear on a yacht cruising in international waters, or perhaps while picking up a latte in Copenhagen. The stuff you hear in every European airport.

M.O.: This style of music frequently incorporates synth pads, which can provide an exotic complement to a track, while also functioning as an effective fill.

Left hand: Playing and sustaining octave roots on beat one.

Right hand: Executing the pattern, in time.

Hot hint: Many other fills are possible here, as well as the opportunity to solo using the G minor scale.

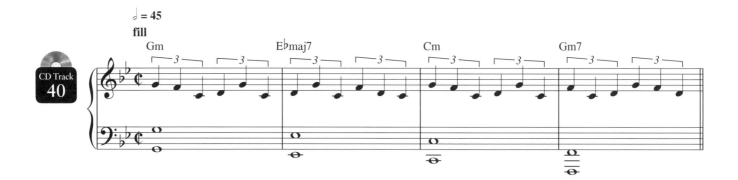

SKA

Instrument: Organ

Key: G major

Keytext: A precursor to rocksteady and reggae, ska originated in Jamaica in the 1950s.

M.O.: This genre is a riot for keyboardists, because we get to lock in with the two and four of the snare, then put it in cruise and let the good times roll! In this example, I'm hitting the changes with short, effective chordal quarter-note stabs.

Left hand: Reaching for a smoothie.

Right hand: Hitting and quitting.

Hot hint: Sometimes the simplest things are the best. Try simply holding out a G over the changes; this works as well. With the organ, one note is all you need.

KEY LESSONS

PRESHOW

"Punctuality is the courtesy of kings."

−King Louis XVIII of France

Wires in place and taped down, equipment nicely laid out, stand(s) strategically placed and secure, space to get the job done sussed out: these are the signs of an orderly and well-planned sonic strategy. It lets the universe, the audience, and yourself know that you mean business and you came to play.

Sometime's it's a pole. Sometime's it's the heat. Sometimes the stage is shaped liked a small trampoline. Whatever it is, when you're out there, adverse and challenging conditions may occur that you simply won't be able control. In those cases, fighting is a waste of energy. Accepting and working with your given stage, overall surroundings, and general environment is your best and only option. Make the most of what's available and roll with it.

In the end, it all comes down to the direct boxes you use. They are the final gatekeeper for what goes out to the studio or live mixer. You can have the most pristine signal flow in the world, but if it hits the wrong coils, it could end up sounding like yesterday's cottage cheese. Be absolutely sure your DIs are hi-fi. (See page 87.)

Everyone loves stereo, especially sound engineers, but don't sweat it. Unless you're listening to the gig through a pair of headphones, chances are that, in a roomful of people, the sound is just going to refract all over the joint anyway. Folks are there to see and hear you play, not to write a review for Deutsche Grammophon.

A good monitor mix, though not absolutely essential for a solid live performance, is nonetheless an invaluable piece of the playing-live puzzle. If you're on a small stage and can already hear your fellow players well, it's less of an issue. But on the bigger stages, where your rhythm guitarist is a football field away, monitors may be your only means to connection. Have an orderly and professional soundcheck. Make one request at a time. Run a loud number for a few bars. If you need any changes, make them one at a time. If not, thank your monitor mixer and exit.

Take a moment before you play to actually thank whatever device or energy you feel is most appropriate to thank for the opportunity to serve others and yourself through music. The universe appreciates a high-five once in a while. In my case, I literally bow to the instrument before I play it. Perhaps a little extreme, but I've never been one to hold back.

Your stage look makes a statement about you. It says, "I'm relaxed." It says, "I'm clueless." It says, "Don't mess with me." In effect, it says anything you want it to say. But be very aware, it's definitely saying something, whether you mean it to or not.

Before you hit, do some pushups or run around or something, anything to get your heart going and your head engaged. Have a pre-game ritual. Work yourself up. Get ready to give 110 percent.

I often refrain from eating before I play. Why? Because after I eat I get sleepy. When I play the keys, I don't want to be sleepy. I want and need to play with maximum force. For me, playing hungry is the best way to go, both literally and spiritually.

SHOWTIME

If you play your parts with conviction and commitment, you will be taken seriously.

The audience is your friend. They want you to succeed. If you're relaxed and having fun, or at least appear to be, they will relax and have fun with you. This is true in 99 percent of the shows you'll play, regardless of the notes that are coming out of the speakers. Don't scowl at the audience or put them down. Have fun with them. Interact. They want you to want them.

When you're out in the field, things happen: you might want to extend a jam a few bars, even though you didn't rehearse it that way, or you might want to end a song early if the vibe isn't working. Or you might want to support someone else's exceptional playing or singing. In any and all cases, it's vital that you maintain constant awareness of the musical work going on all around you.

A key irony: the less you play, the better you sound!

You and the audience are traveling together in a car. The audience is in the back seat. But make no mistake, you're driving. When you're taking a musical turn it's because you, singularly and collectively as a band, have decided to take it. Not the audience. They are looking to you for sonic guidance.

Sometimes I find myself getting so wrapped up in the playing that I momentarily forget about the existence of anything else around me. Whenever that happens, I must remind myself to come back down to earth and listen to what everyone else is doing. Then I ask myself: Does my playing support this? Am I taking up too much sonic space? Too little?

There's a good reason Little Richard, Jerry Lee Lewis, and Keith Emerson are riveting live personalities and it's something entirely separate from their incredible chops. It's their showmanship, their love of performance, and complete and total trust of their physical instincts in the moment.

You dropped the maracas. Your keyboard stand fell over. Your mic stand just did a 180. Your secret retort? You meant to do that! Follow the universe into the depths of humility and embarrassment with an open heart and outstretched elbows. Don't analyze what happened, dive into the morass and make it yours. Pick your keyboard back up, twirl around and give the audience the "rock on" sign. The place will go bananas!

Keyboard solos are tricky. You've got to pace them so they develop nicely, each note building upon the previous. But you've also got to get out of the way fast once you've spoken your piece. Generally it's best to leave them wanting more. Remember, guitars never get old and are never too loud. Keys, by contrast, have a tendency to be everyone's least favorite uncle if left unchecked. Be a considerate player.

Your charge is to perform and raise spirits. One spirit. 10. 100. 1,000. 10,000. 100,000. 1,000,000. It doesn't matter. Put on the same show regardless. It's good karma.

Here's an interesting and unavoidable key truth: the boards have a tendency to get buried in the overall mix. You can spend hours and hours trying to figure out why this is, and I have. But at the end of the night, it's still the same thing. So play your parts, rock out, be true to your school, and don't be surprised when your friends say they couldn't hear you.

Just like good bread, manners are something that everyone appreciates but rarely mentions. They shouldn't have to. Remember, everyone has a story. Be cool. Give folks the benefit of the doubt, and work together toward the common goal of making people happy with music. Saying "thanks"—to your audience, bandmates, and crew—is ridiculously easy, effortlessly classy, and absolutely essential.

At the end of the night, help load out the equipment. It's all the same gear.

STUDIO

Studio playing is like listening to every sound under an electronic microscope-for-your-ears. Each waveform acts as is its own universe. It offers many different roots to the same sonically realized tree. Sometimes it's good to have your parts well thought out in advance. Other times, the less you analyze, the more appropriate your parts are to the overall track. Ultimately, as a musician, the studio provides an opportunity to contribute, in your own unique and beautiful way, to the making of some Joyous Noise.

Playing in time, playing in tune, playing in tempo, playing in line; in this cloistered and sacred space of creation, nobody else can see you, nobody else knows you, nobody else cares about you. They will know you only by your Trail of Shred.

Studio IOU: For teaching me the fine art of serving the song with sounds and silences.

Always have a plan of action before you start the session. What is the ultimate goal of the day? Figure that out, focus your energy, and stick to it.

Just because your brand new shiny happy keytoy comes out of the box perfectly tuned to A 440 doesn't necessarily mean that everyone else in the band has chosen that particular frequency as their common tuning model! Always check your tuning with the track before rolling a note.

Your DI box is your link to the outside world. It is ultimately the most important part of your signal chain because it is the last unit to touch it, and therefore your last chance to boost and improve your tone. If possible, get yourself a high quality box. This can literally make the difference between jarring noise and dulcet tones by optimizing your signal-to-noise ratio and distortion levels while adding overall warmth and line level to your signal.

Regarding stereo vs. mono: some parts and instruments actually sound better in mono, depending on their mix placement and overall sonic function. Many classic synths don't even offer stereo outputs, while artful mic placement on acoustic instruments, especially piano and organ, can foster effective results in both mediums.

If you can somehow finagle things so that the keys are added last, I highly recommend it—unless, of course, it's a live band-to-tape situation. How do you know which instrument and what parts will best serve the song? As a keyboardist, in my experience, it's very difficult to tell until you hear everything together. Only then can one fully analyze the sonic spectrum and discern how best to musically enable the piece you're working on. You can then make a fully informed musical choice and direct it with well-focused execution. If time, schedule, or other elements force you to record early, do your best to get as clear a picture as possible of the songwriter's and/or producer's vision of what the final mix will sound and feel like, then proceed with these thoughts in mind.

Studio playing affords one the opportunity to audition as many different parts, ideas, and musical concepts as can be imagined. There is nothing to be lost from trying out a new idea. It will be immediately evident whether or not it's the right move to make.

Laying out is the keyboard player's secret sonic weapon; it makes the parts you do choose to play sound that much more powerful. As a musician, but particularly as a keyboardist, you have the power and responsibility of musically saying just enough. Sometimes this involves playing like a windmill in heat. Most often, however, I've found that keeping the part simple and understated is the most efficient means to this end. Less equals more.

In some cases, you'll be asked to emulate other existing acoustic instruments—i.e., "Can you make this part sound like an oboe?" There's a vast array of libraries, samplers, plug-ins, and MIDI controllers available to choose from out there, and what sounds "real" to someone is a very subjective thing. Audition as many of them as possible, then choose your weapon. You may get pretty close, but the bottom line is that a keyboard can't sound exactly like another instrument, only that instrument can really sound exactly like that instrument. Huh?

What we *can* do, once we've found the right sound, is play the parts as if they were being played by real players who are playing the real instruments. Range and instrument-specific technique are two ways to accomplish this. Some sonorities seem to work well, especially if doubled by a real instrument (strings), while others have a tendency to consistently give themselves away as fake (horns). As John Paul Jones said regarding the strings and Mellotron parts on Led Zeppelin's "Kashmir":

The secret of successful keyboard string parts is to play only the parts that a real string section would play. That is, one line for the first violins, one line for the second violins, one for violas, one for the cellos, one for basses. Some divided parts are allowed, but keep them to a minimum. Think melodically.

The most important thing I've ever picked up in the studio as far as keys are concerned: the softer the keyboards are in the final mix, the more present they will sound to the listener. Conversely, the louder the keyboards are placed in the final, they more overbearing and intrusive they will sound. It's sort of a "less-is-more" last laugh that nature has with us boards-bearers. Bottom line: Play less and they will adore you, turn it down and they won't ignore you.

PLAYING IN THE BAND
Tales from the ripped.

RICHARD CHEESE

I had the privilege and opportunity to play the coasts, Vegas, and other various and sundry hot spots with Mark Davis, a.k.a. Richard Cheese. With Chuck Byler on drums and Chris Monaco on bass, we'd hit the kids hard with killer comedy and rapid-fire ricochets of righteous raucousness. It was all too much, a total blast. And while Mark made plenty of time for improvised bits, the show consisted in large part of well-rehearsed and thoughtfully arranged two-to-three minute tunes that had been painstakingly and exhaustively pieced together through many hours of rehearsal. As a bandleader, Mark considered it his mission to ensure high energy, laughs, and killer chopage in every minute of every set we played. The lesson I learned from him: Be prepared. Have it all together and locked, memorized, and effortlessly in your fingers before you let anyone else hear a note.

CHICAGO

Working with some of the best, most talented, and versatile actors, improvisers, writers, and performers in the nation was an enormous thrill and musical highlight for me. "Work" consisted of making up songs and scores, night after night for hundreds and hundreds of enthusiastic audience members. At the Annoyance Theater, Second City, and ImprovOlympic theaters, I was given free reign to musically go where no human had gone before. I gleefully followed the action, mood, and atmosphere of given scenes, sonically emoted with the performers to build climaxes and accentuate pauses, and improvised songs and musical asides on-the-fly. It was an accompanist's dream.

Who were some of these wacky people with whom I had the honor and privilege of working? Too many beautiful souls to mention them all, but here are just a few:

Matt Besser, Joe Bill, Brian Blondell, Tom Booker, Kerry Brown, Beth Cahill, Mike Coleman, Kevin Dorff, Rachel Dratch, Jennifer Estlin, Jon Favreau, Kate Flannery, Neil Flynn, Rich Fulcher, Ed Furman, Jeff Garlin, Ian Gomez, James Grace, Noah Gregoropoulos, Charna Halpern, Eric Hoffman, Jackie Hoffman, Melanie Hutsell, Jay Johnston, Pat Finn, David Koechner, Jay Leggett, Jodi Lennon, Madeline Long, Jane Lynch, Jack McBrayer, Brian McCann, Michael McCarthy, Adam McKay, Martin de Maat, Susan Messing, Seth Meyers, Mick Napier, Brett Paesel, David Pasquesi, Amy Poehler, David Razowsky, Andy Richter, Scot Robinson, Mitch Rouse, Gabrielle Sanalitro, Faith Soloway, Jill Soloway, Brian Stack, Mark Sutton, Rich Talarico, Pat Towne, Matt Walsh, Becky Thyre, Marisol Torres, Ben Zook, Jim Zulevic... among many, many significant others.

They were all a blast to work with, and I learned something from each of them, including—but not limited to—the fine art of pacing, the value of total commitment to the moment, and the magic of group-mind singularity. Good times!

COMEDYSPORTZ

Back in the '80s I was involved with an outfit called ComedySportz. It was my first experience with accompanying live improvised theater. What a great time! The "anything goes" atmosphere combined with a group of exceptionally talented performers and musicians that included Mark Hervey, Brian Kapell, Josh Lewis, Mike Rock, Chris Tallman, and loads of others, made it a glorious introduction to the wondrous worlds of improvisation and proved to be ideal training for Chicago.

THE GOMERS

I've been playing with the Gomers for over 20 years. They are all great friends and musical brethren. They taught me that nothing beats making joyous noise with folks you love.

THE GROOVE

My first high school band. Chris Laine, Paul Lottridge, Eric Hailman and I won over gyms and even opened for Los Lobos back in the day. The Groove taught me that it doesn't matter how you roll in everyday life: If you can truly lay it down onstage, you'll gain much respect from your peers.

KEN LONNQUIST

Ken is nationally known singer/songwriter based in Madison, Wisconsin. I've been playing with him since I was 16, and it was his patience and encouragement that first gave me the confidence to improvise. One of his many lessons for me: don't censor. If the universe leads you to say or play something that you haven't heard before or hadn't planning on doing, you are the only one who knows that. The audience certainly doesn't, and the other players may or may not, depending on what's for dinner. Follow the path upon which fate or serendipity has placed you, commit fully to your sound, build upon it, and move fearlessly onward and upward.

WILLY PORTER

An amazing musician, producer, and songwriter. Apart from performing set material, he is not afraid to venture headlong into the improvised unknown, fearlessly and full of fun. Here are two things Willy utilizes to great effect in his live shows:

1. Dynamics: Shhh, what was that? A pin dropping? No! It was the guitar playing a whisper-quiet and undeniably effective solo! Cool! Getting quiet, grooving with that, and enjoying the ride up and down from full rock-out level to pianissimo will make the full-throttle parts of the show rock just that much harder!

2. Trust: Willy trusts his players to trust him, both as a bandleader and band member. His players trust him to trust each of them to do what they do well. This mutual trust-fest provides an attitude of confidence... and trust. As with any team, it is only when the players feel both the confidence in their individual gifts *and* the awareness of what their team-mates have to offer that the group can realize its full potential to function well as a whole.

The included clip, "Welcome to San Francisco," was recorded live and unscripted.

 "Welcome to San Francisco"

JOE PUERTA

I've been privileged to work with Joe Puerta for many years at his recording studio, The Exchange, in Milwaukee, Wisconsin. He has been there and done that. In addition to his seminal work with Ambrosia and Bruce Hornsby and the Range, he is an astoundingly talented producer, composer, bassist, and vocalist in his own right. Immediately upon witnessing him play, sing, and produce, I knew that he "had it." His illustrious career did not happen by accident—his million dollar chops shine with every musical move he makes. For me, Joe is a living embodiment of the maxim "You know it when you hear it."

CLYDE STUBBLEFIELD

When I was in my mid-20s I was lucky, honored, and privileged to play in a band with the legendary super-sampled funky drummer himself, Mr. Clyde Stubblefield. The name of the band was Green Eggs and Sam. Clyde opened my mind and my ears to the unlimited rhythmical contributions the keys can make by literally changing how I perceived them: my outlook shifted from considering them stringed instruments to thinking of them as percussive. While the former school encouraged development of individual tone—which is vital and particularly suited to classical music, especially the solo repertoire—rhythmic playing fostered overall groove, execution of complementary parts, and an approach that generally promoted group thinking over focus on the individual. In my musical vernacular, this M.O. has become indispensable in my ongoing effort to make a consistently strong, solid melodic contribution.

In 2009, I had the opportunity to play a couple of live duo gigs with Clyde. Completely improvised and lacking in any formal structure, we would slide instantly and interchangeably from one groove into another, making up melody lines, lyrics, beginnings, and endings as we went. It was a wonderful, magical experience, and increased my already all-encompassing appreciation for this incredible man; a vital, ever-present, world changing musical dynamo with a flexible and engaged mind, invisible ego, and heart of gold. When I grow up, I want to be just like him.

CONCLUSION
Measured chaos.

WHAT HAVE WE LEARNED ON THE SHOW TONIGHT DAVE?

It's joyous to groove and to make people dance.

Playing the keys will give you a chance.

Push down those pedals, pull out those stops.

Put some French dip in those hippity hops.

Have a good time, get out of the way,

You're just one in the cast of this playful played play,

So lay down your lines, have some good times,

Pack up your gear and try not to whine.

Prince.

You know it's time to move on when you've learned all you can learn and given all you can give.

Gratitude is the attitude.

The path to finding your own sound begins with emulating the sounds of players that you admire. Mimicry's not gimmickry. As your sphere of knowledge grows, you will find yourself combining all these various influences in new and exciting ways. You will then be on your way to creating your own original, unique sound.

KEY LIMITATIONS

· Keyboards aren't guitars.

· Some of them weigh a lot.

· People can't always see you playing them.

· Mobility restriction.

· Hard to victory-throw to roadie at end of show.

First the songs were free. Then Edison invented some stuff and for a while the means of production and distribution of music could be controlled. Now they're free again. Live performance is back. Be an analog kid in a digital world.

Many accidentals happen on purpose.

Showing up is half the battle.

TOP 10 REASONS KEYBOARDS ARE THE COOLEST

1. They are the cherry on the sundae of rock.

2. They are the sparkle in the sonic eye.

3. They are the "yes and..."

4. They take it higher.

5. They bring it down.

6. They spice it up.

7. They glue it together.

8. They're keyriffic.

9. Everyone tunes to them.

10. You never have to worry about running out of breath while playing.

Live to rock, rock to live.

Hear the need and fill it.

Less is more.

Learn from the best, then do the rest.

Trust your hands. They know what to do.

The doorman at Joe's Pub in New York City shook my hand after a show and told me I blew him away. Highest compliment I've ever received.

I saw Bernie Worrell play with Jerry Harrison at Headliners in Madison, Wisconsin in 1983. Couldn't speak for a week.

When you're in the zone, you can float above your body and watch yourself play.

I prefer to hear the music of Kurt Weill played on a Kurzweil.

"Music is the space between the notes."

   –Claude Debussy

"It's not the notes you play, it's the notes you don't play."

   –Miles Davis

"Kabanga!"   (Zulu for "Imagination!")

Q'S QUICKSTART

- Blues scales and rhythm changes ("I Got Rhythm") in every key.

- Learn your favorite songs note by note.

- Keep your hands relaxed, play in time, play in tune. Musicality always beats technicality.

NOTES FROM TERRY

Years ago my friend Terry Landry, a multi-Grammy winning saxophonist based in L.A., shared some thoughts about his experiences in the music business and what he learned from them. I'll conclude with some of his pearls of wisdom:

- Follow your heart, but cover your ass. Plan and care for your finances.

- Build a network of industry people, musicians and otherwise, who are in your corner. This is money in the bank.

- Anytime you depend on someone else for your livelihood or fulfillment, you will eventually get screwed, 100 percent of the time. Put your own thing together.

- Do your best in whatever situation you find yourself. Always continue to learn your craft as well as possible.

- Pursue others' projects for their artistic merit.

- Establish a circle of cool people who stimulate your creativity and make you feel good about yourself. Peers in your ever-widening circle will like having their buddies along for the ride.

- Become a master of communication. Be thorough, and say what needs to be said in a way that inspires.

- Be easygoing, flexible, and professional, but stick to your guns. Learn from everyone and every situation, but have the courage to be yourself.

- Work with people you love.

KEY TERMS

A cappella: Unaccompanied singing.

Accidental: A sign to the left of a note, either a sharp, flat, or natural. See individual key terms listings.

Arpeggio: Playing the notes of a chord one at a time, "broken chord" style.

Bar: See *measure*.

Blue note: A note outside of prescribed scale, typically added for color.

Bridge: In popular music styles, generally the third part of a song that is neither the verse nor the chorus. Sometimes referred to as the "middle eight," because the typical duration is eight measures.

Bubble: A playing technique in reggae in which the keyboard plays offbeats (the "and" of the beat) opposite downbeats, producing a "bubble" effect.

Chord: Three or more different notes sounding simultaneously. Chords are often built in stacked third intervals.

Chord inversion: A chord rearranged so that the root is no longer on the bottom.

Chorus: The most important, memorable, repeated part of song. ("Don't bore us. Get to the chorus.")

Chromatic scale: Twelve ascending/descending half-steps (semi-tones).

Clef: The sign at beginning of staff designating pitch. Treble clef (right hand) and bass clef (left hand) are most common with keyboard notation.

Clone: Keyboard specifically designed to sound like an already existing instrument.

Comping: Musical slang for *accompaniment*, i.e, playing behind/supporting featured player or vocalist.

Counterpoint: Two or more melody lines sounding simultaneously.

Diatonic scale: Major or minor scale (eight tones).

DI (direct input) box: Connects high impedance/line-level signal (1/4") to low impedance/mic-level signal (XLR).

Dominant: The fifth note of a scale.

Drone: A long, sustained note.

Dynamic marking: A marking in the music signifying how loud or soft to play:

    ppp   pianississimo; very, very soft

    pp   pianissimo; very soft

    p   piano; soft

    mp   mezzo piano; moderately soft

    mf   mezzo forte; moderately loud

    f   forte; loud

    ff   fortissimo; very loud

    fff   fortississimo; very, very loud

Enharmonic equivalents: Alternative names for the same note. For example, the note C♯ is enharmonic to the note D♭.

Equal temperament: A system of keyboard tuning that divides the octave into 12 equal half-steps, allowing one to play in all keys without sounding perceptively out of tune.

Fundamental: The note upon which a chord is based.

Glissando: Rapid sliding of notes, typically played by dragging a hand or fingernail up or down the keyboard.

Grace note: A note of very short duration that is "squeezed in" before another note.

Interval: The distance in pitch between two notes.

Instrumentation: The instruments used in an ensemble.

Inversion: See *chord inversion*.

Key: The key indicates the main note (tonic) of the piece, and which scale the piece is based on, subject to any accidentals in the music.

Key signature: A series of sharps or flats at beginning of a piece of music indicating which key you are in.

Measure: A group of beats set apart by two consecutive horizontal barlines.

Meter: The grouping of beats (i.e., four counts per bar, etc.).

MIDI: Stands for Musical Instrument Digital Interface; the protocol used by keyboard, computers, and other musical instruments to communicate with one another.

Midi controller: A keyboard specifically designed to drive external MIDI gear with no—or limited—internal sounds.

Motif (motive): A brief musical idea; it can be melodic, harmonic, or rhythmic—or all threee.

Modulation: Change of key within a composition.

Natural: A sign placed before a note to cancel a sharp or flat.

Octave: The interval distance between any note to the next-occurring note of the same name, either higher or lower on the keyboard.

Ostinato: A clearly defined, repeated musical phrase.

Phrase: A defined melodic musical line.

Pickup measure: An incomplete measure at the beginning of a song, used if the piece does not begin on beat 1.

Plug-in: A software extension providing virtual instruments and/or effects.

Rack mount: Portable version of synthesizer, sampler, or other instrument with guts only, no keyboard; driven via external midi controller.

Ritardando: A gradual slowing of tempo.

Root: The fundamental note of a chord; for example, the root of a D major triad is the note D.

Scale: A sequence of notes built using a specific set of intervals, extending from any given note to its octave.

Seventh chord: Fundamental plus third, fifth, and seventh.

Sequence: A melodic idea that is repeated at different pitch levels.

Soft synth (virtual instrument): A computer-based instrument triggered internally or via MIDI.

Staff: Five horizontal lines and four included spaces upon which music is written.

Tempo: The speed (i.e., slow, moderate, fast) at which a composition is played.

Timbre: Also known as "tone color." For example, a flute, oboe, and trumpet all playing the same note are said to produce different "timbres." Acoustically, timbre has to do with the combination of fundamental tone and corresponding overtones (harmonics).

Time signature: A fraction-like sign at beginning of the piece indicating how many beats are in each measure (top number) and what rhythmic value is assigned to the beat (bottom number).

Tonic: The first and main note of key.

Triad: A chord consisting of three notes.

Triplet: Three notes played in the space normally occupied by two.

Tritone: An interval spanning three whole tones (augmented 4th, diminished 5th), thus dividing the octave. Also known as the "devil's interval" (*diabolus in musica*).

Unison: Identical or octave-duplicated pitches.

Vamp: To repeat a selected phrase or portion of song.

Verse: The portion of a song that usually precedes the chorus.

Whole-tone scale: A scale consisting only of whole steps; great for dreams and flashbacks.

Woodshedding: Saying goodbye to your friends and loved ones, grabbing your axe, and heading for the hills.

CD TRACK LISTING

1. Major Scales

2. Minor Scales

3. Blues Scales

4. Chromatic Scales

5. Inversions

6. Comping #1: performed by Footlong

7. Comping #2: excerpt from "Skirt Dance"
written by Alex Wood

8. Comping #3: excerpt from "Dude You Rock"
written by Gordon Ranney
performed by The Gomers

9. Fills #1: excerpt from "Angela"
written by Mark Croft

10. Fills #2: excerpt from "Mr. Sorry"
written by Alex Wood
lead vocal by Kiah Kalimese-Walker

11. Minor Blues

12. Blues Shuffle

13. Up-tempo Blues

14. Standard Blues

15. Standard Country

16. Up-tempo Country

17. Mid-tempo Country

18. Roadhouse Country

19. Straight Ahead Jazz

20. Fusion

21. Lounge Jazz

22. Smooth Jazz

23. Standard Latin

24. Bossa

25. Samba

26. Beguine

27. Hip Hop

28. Funk

29. Funk Rock

30. Trip Hop

31. Motown

32. Soul

33. Hard Rock

34. Soft Rock

35. Medium Rock

36. '50s Rock

37. Party Rock

38. Reggae

39. Up-tempo Reggae

40. International

41. Ska

42. "Welcome to San Francisco"
written and performed by
Dave Adler and Willy Porter

All keyboards performed by Dave Adler.

All music used by permission.

Footlong is: Jeff Hill, guitar; Dave Moore, bass; Bill "The Myth" Smith, drums; Dave Adler, keyboards.

Recorded July 1997 at Martyrs, Chicago, IL. Engineered by Ray Quinn.

The Gomers are: Biff Blumfumgagnge, strings; Geoff Brady, drums; Steve Burke, guitar; Mark Hervey, guitar; Gordon Ranney, bass; Gregg Rullman, drums; Andy Wallman, vox and percussion; Dave Adler, keyboards.

Recorded March 2010 at Smart Studios, Madison, WI. Engineered by Mike Zirkel and Beau Sorenson.

Additional recording August 2010 at DNA Studios, Madison, WI. Engineered by Mark Whitcomb.

Mark Croft   www.markcroftmusic.com

Dave Adler   www.daveadler.com

DNA Studios   www.dnamusiclabs.com

Footlong   www.myspace.com/dhamba8

The Gomers   www.thegomers.net

Martyrs   www.martyrslive.com

Willy Porter   www.willyporter.com

Smart Studios   www.smartgeeks.com

ACKNOWLEDGMENTS

All of these people, in their own unique and vital ways, were instrumental in the creation of this book:

Hilde Adler, Julius Adler, Laly Adler, Mariluz Adler, J. Mark Baker, Bob Bell, Ellie Bell, Biff Blumfumgagnge, Steve Burke, John Calarco, Mark Croft, Beverly Haberman, Ted Jackson, Tony Jarvis, Dale Kushner, Ken Lonnquist, Jeane McMahon, Lonnie Nofzinger, Georgia O'Keefe, Willy Porter, Marvin Rabin, Rhoda Rabin, John Rafoth, Gordon Ranney, Jeanette Ranney, Jeff Schroedl, Kathy Sih, Paulo Steagall, Jody Wall, Andy Wallman, Alex Wood, Mike Zirkel.

I thank each of them!

ABOUT THE AUTHOR

Photo by James Conway

Milwaukee, Wisconsin; July 2010

DAVE ADLER is a composer, producer, and keyboard player. After serving as a music director for Chicago's Second City, Annoyance, and ImprovOlympic theaters, he completed the graduate program at the University of Southern California, specializing in composition for motion pictures and television. From there, he scored the first season of Comedy Central's *Upright Citizens Brigade*.

Next, he teamed up with swing savants Richard Cheese and Lounge Against the Machine. Acting as musical director and arranger, the group's Sinatra-styled renditions of alternative rock hits drew critical praise, national airplay, and record-setting crowds at live appearances across the country. Highlights included appearances on NBC, MTV, FOX, and CNN, as well as a featured big band arrangement for Universal Pictures' *Dawn of the Dead* remake.

Following an album and Icelandic tour with former Sugar Cubes drummer Siggi Baldursson, Adler composed and produced the original score for *Chicago Boricua*. The independent feature premiered at New York's Tribeca Film Festival and received national distribution through Screen Media/Universal. Adler then teamed up with renowned guitarist/singer-songwriter Willy Porter to co-produce *Available Light*, named one of the year's best releases by *Performing Songwriter* magazine.

Adler's additional clients include Apple, the Discovery Channel, A&E, HBO, and Mattel. He is also a proud member of the Gomers, the official house band of Madison, Wisconsin.